ADD

. . . the facts,
. . . the fables,
. . . hope for your family

ADD

... the facts,
... the fables,
... hope for your family

by Theresa Lamson

Vital Issues Press

Vital Issues Press
P.O. Box 53788
Lafayette, Louisiana 70505

Library of Congress Card Catalog Number
96-060585
ISBN 1-56384-121-5

Printed in the U.S.A.

What is written in this book is based on the author's personal experience with ADD and her research of the disorder and, as such, is not to be considered medical advice. What is explained in its content is not meant to be a substitute for medical treatment of ADD, and any medications or forms of therapy mentioned should only be approached with the assistance of a physician. The reader should consult a qualified health care professional concerning matters relating to health and particularly with respect to any symptoms that may require diagnosis or medical attention.

Dedication

This book is dedicated
to Bob and Vi Jones, my Vineyard Family,
and the members of my natural family who
carry me in their prayers daily for the sake of
the Kingdom.
May your inheritance in the Lord be
evident to all in this life and
in the life to come.

Contents

Preface

Having been a pastor's wife for nineteen years, my adult spiritual life has consisted of seeking ways to lead, guide, and nurture the flock of God, as well as birth lambs along the way. This has given my husband and me the chance to be exposed to a wide variety of personalities and assist Christians in dealing with a broad spectrum of circumstances. By the grace of God, rather than developing pastoral "burnout" from the strain, we became people of prayer, intense Bible study, and in-depth researchers of both natural and spiritual material. As such, I suppose we shouldn't be surprised at what we have come to learn concerning the currently popular condition known as ADD, and, yet, we have been caught by surprise in discovering the potential for Christ's healing power to move into the lives of God's people by identifying previously unrealized factors.

While there will always remain with us those individuals who are looking for reasons to excuse their behavior, latching onto any newly discovered condition that will justify their actions, I am firmly convinced that there are people dedicated to personal excellence in Christ who have been frustrated in their efforts by unrecognized obstacles. Where the former make us skeptical of any new diagnosis and its relationship to Christianity, for the sake of the latter we must remain open to new discoveries and be willing to examine them from the full counsel of God revealed to us in Scripture.

My desire in writing this book is to give Christians the current information available on the natural manifestations of the condition, a biblical perspective of its root cause, practical understanding of how Christians with ADD have been hindered from achieving their goal of excellence in Christ, and spiritual guidelines that will create a "pathway" for the healing power of Jesus Christ to break down previously unidentified barriers. This will lead to greater health and productivity in the Kingdom of God. In my attempt to accomplish this, I also hope to challenge the attitude of viewing ADD as a "disorder," and bring people to the place of acknowledging the aspects of this condition that qualify it as a gift from God—a gift that will indeed blossom into fruitfulness when understood and nurtured in God's presence.

I want to thank my sister, Mary, for her courage in sending me *Driven to Distraction*; my husband, Gary, for his writing assistance and support; my first professional ADD contact and dear friend Cindy DeVall of DeVall Counseling Services; and the two follow-up physicians, Dr. Brent Prather and Dr. Michael Melancon, for introducing our family to the "ADD world" with kindness, balance, insight, integrity, encouragement, and hope. I also want to thank author Thom Hartmann for his availability and words of encouragement to me throughout my development of this project.

I pray that the words I write will be as much a blessing to you as these individuals have been to our family and that Christ will be magnified in your life to a greater degree through what you learn about yourself and others as a result of this work.

1. An Experience in Discovery

Blessed is the man who finds wisdom, the man who gains understanding.

—Proverbs 3:13

When my sister in Canby, Oregon, sent me a copy of *Driven to Distraction* by Drs. Hallowell and Ratey, I had no way of knowing the spiritual journey on which it would send me. As with many of the spiritual experiences we go through, I went into the mode of "discovery," gaining new perceptions and insights about myself, my family, and my extended spiritual family, receiving fresh applications of Scripture for spiritual growth in Christ.

By the time I was a few chapters into *Distraction*, I was understanding much of the material from a spiritual perspective. I felt as though God was teaching me something. Quite frankly, the only exposure I previously had with this condition was in knowing a family whose child consistently misbehaved and caused distraction to others. The parents blamed the child's behavior on this ADD "thing," which I had a hard time believing since the family wasn't doing the basics of providing a loving, secure, nurturing environment for the child. I was convinced it was largely an excuse for their lack of parenting and became ambivalent about ADDers and their cause. Obviously that has changed.

After reading *Driven to Distraction*, I began to hunt for whatever was available on the subject. It was a great disappointment to find out how little was available in Christian bookstores and surprising how much was available in the secular marketplace. I read a wide range of works on the subject and, in the course of my study, was exposed to the critics of ADD, who have some valid concerns and viewpoints. This helped me to develop a more solid and balanced base of understanding concerning a proper Christian response to the ADD community.

In the secular realm, recent years have brought about the dawning of a new era of understanding human behaviors which is touching and affecting every related profession. ADD is seemingly being propelled along by the crest of that wave. Although it is currently a somewhat popular condition, the "discovery" aspect has been lengthy and complicated. Several of the books I read chronicled the history of learning and behavior disorders dating back to 1902, relating stories of doctors dealing with children who had symptoms of chronic emotional disturbance, defiance, restlessness, and excessive distractibility.

The "condition" has been through a maze of labels, from the early MBD (minimal brain dysfunction), to the hyperkinetic syndrome, hyperactive child syndrome, eventually evolving into the more specific labels of learning and behavior disorders, learning disabilities, dyslexia and so on. These initial understandings focused on the external evidence rather than the mechanics of the brain. In the 1970s, the concept of "attention deficits" emerged, which eventually gave way to the term *Attention Deficit Disorder* in 1980. The correct current diagnostic label is attention deficit hyperactive disorder, which Dr. Hallowell claims is an imperfect label since many people with ADD are more dreamy and quiet than hyperactive.[1]

Understanding of the condition progressed in a meandering fashion through an endless maze of speculation. Was it caused by parental failure, moral weakness, or genetic weakness? Throughout the widely variant schools of theory, there remained the persistent consideration that there was a biological factor causing, if not at least exacerbating, the condition. Yet, equally persistent was the view of ADD as a fabricated affliction manufactured to justify rebellious children and unfit parents, or a "myth" created by frustrated teachers trying to instruct children within the limiting confines of the educational system. No one will deny that there are rebellious children, unfit parents, and frustrated educators, but couldn't there also be some truths concerning ADD behaviors that could enable us to grow in our ability to guide and nurture our children?

As I share with you my discovery of ADD, I want to begin by looking at the current perception of what ADD is. In its simplest definition, the condition of ADD is thought to stem from malfunctions within the brain and central nervous system, which affect and/or produce behavior responses that challenge the structure of our social and educational environments. The criteria for child diagnosis of the condition is outlined in the *Diagnostic and Statistic Manual of the American Psychiatric Association*, better known as DSM-IV-R. It consists of the following:

• Diagnostic criteria for attention deficit/ hyperactivity disorder

A. Either 1. or 2.

1. Six (or more) of the following symptoms of inattention have persisted for at least six months to a degree that is maladaptive and inconsistent with developmental level:

Inattention

a) Often fails to give close attention to details or makes careless mistakes in schoolwork, work, or other activities.

b) Often has difficulty sustaining attention in tasks or play activities.

c) Often does not seem to listen when spoken to directly.

d) Often does not follow through on instructions and fails to finish schoolwork, chores, or duties in the workplace (not due to oppositional behavior or failure to understand instructions).

e) Often has difficulty organizing tasks and activities.

f) Often avoids, dislikes, or is reluctant to engage in tasks that require sustained mental effort (such as schoolwork or homework).

g) Often loses things necessary for tasks or activities (e.g., toys, school assignments, pencils, books, or tools).

h) Often easily distracted by extraneous stimuli.

i) Often forgetful in daily activities.

2. Six (or more) of the following symptoms of **hyperactivity-impulsivity** have persisted for at least six months to a degree that is maladaptive and inconsistent with developmental level:

Hyperactivity

a) Often fidgets with hands or feet or squirms in seat.

b) Often leaves seat in classroom or in other situations in which remaining seated is expected.

c) Often runs about or climbs excessively in situations in which it is inappropriate (in adolescents or adults, may be limited to subjective feelings of restlessness).

d) Often has difficulty playing or engaging in leisure activities quietly.

e) Often "on the go" or often acts as if "driven by a motor."

f) Often talks excessively.

Impulsivity

g) Often blurts out answers before questions have been completed.

h) Often has difficulty awaiting turn.

i) Often interrupts or intrudes on others (e.g., butts into conversations or games).

B. Some hyperactive-impulsive inattentive symptoms that caused impairment were present before the age of seven years.

C. Some impairment from the symptoms is present in two or more settings (e.g., at school [or work] and at home).

D. There must be clear evidence of clinically significant impairment in social, academic, or occupational functioning.

E. The symptoms do not occur exclusively during the course of a pervasive developmental disorder, schizophrenia, or other psychotic disorder, and are not better accounted for by another mental disorder (e.g., mood disorder, anxiety disorder, dissociative disorder, or a personality disorder).

Code based on type:

314.01 Attention deficit hyperactivity disorder, combined type: if both criteria A1 and A2 are met for the past six months.

314.00 Attention deficit hyperactivity disorder, predominantly inattentive type: if criterion A1 is met but criterion A2 is not met for the past six months.

314.01 Attention deficit hyperactivity disorder, predominantly hyperactive-impulsive

type: if criterion A2 is met but criterion A1
is not met for the past six months.

Coding note: For individuals (especially
adolescents and adults) who currently have
symptoms that no longer meet full criteria,
"In Partial Remission" should be specified.

After reading through this criteria, two
thoughts might have popped into your mind: First
of all, how can these symptoms be related to functions within the brain? Secondly, so many children would fit into this description it's ridiculous!

Let's begin with the first thought. I'm not a
brain expert, but several of the works I've read
delved fairly deeply into the workings of the brain.
It was fascinating to learn so much about brain
function. Allow me to condense for you the most
important information related to brain function
as related to this condition. I'll attempt to do so
without being overly technical!

There are biochemical connections and inter-
actions going on in our brains constantly. Their
patterns of operations directly affect who we are
as individuals and the operation of our natural
talents and gifts. Extensive studies by the likes of
Alan Zametkin and his associates at the National
Institutes of Mental Health have produced substantial evidence that blood flow throughout the
different areas of the brain are different in people
with ADD, leading to the theory that the condition is directly linked to activities within the brain.
Drs. Hallowell and Ratey explain it as a possible
dysregulation of that chemistry, producing an
effect similar to "a dance where one misstep by
one partner creates a misstep by the other, which
creates another misstep by the first. Before they

know it, these dance partners are out of step not just with each other but with the music and who is to say how it happened?"[2]

An important part of brain function takes place in what are called the prefrontal and premotor regions, in which area is the primary regulator of behaviors. This particular area receives its input from the lower brain. Studies have revealed that the brains of people with ADD transport less chemicals from this lower area to the frontal area. The frontal area processes knowledge and sensory information, coordinates attention function, and initiates courses of behavior. In recognizing this, one can easily conclude that a lower level of chemical stimulation to this area can produce the symptoms listed for us in the DSM-IV-R. Think of it. Kids unable to mentally conceive when it is appropriate to speak and be silent, are mentally overwhelmed by the many daily tasks that need their attention, and emotionally distraught by their inability to remember incidentals that seem so easy for everyone else to remember. The theory of specific activities within the brain which affects behaviors doesn't seem so far-fetched after all! As methods of investigation and research continue to rapidly develop, these theories will become clear to everyone.

Then we have the second concern—"so many children would fit into this description it's ridiculous!" This is probably the biggest concern, and rightfully so. After all, the behaviors described in the DSM-IV-R criteria can be produced by a wide variety of factors other than brain activity. Consider the following elements and their affect on a child's ability to focus and manifest "normal" be-

havior. All of them are quite common in the lives
of children today:

> tumultuous home life
> children of divorced parents
> poor diets and nutrition
> lack of physical exercise
> lack of attention given to emotional needs

These are just a few of the modern difficulties
for children that can produce ADD type behaviors. A similar idea was espoused by radio and TV
reporter Paul Harvey in his article on learning
disorders in which he states that they are not illnesses to be cured but conditions to be corrected.[3]

In addition to the difficulty posed by considering the role one's environment plays in affecting behaviors, we are faced with the dilemma that
professional clinicians can vary widely in their diagnostic practices. Although many of those diagnosing the disorder use similar tests and procedures, there isn't any standardized rating scale or
required set of tests and questions for the evaluation process. Clinicians are dependent on their
own research and ability to make judgments on
where individuals fall in the arrayal of "disorders."
They have to rely heavily on the reports of a
child's various caregivers, which are subject to
personal interpretation, making inaccuracy of facts
a plausible concern.

I am keenly aware of the potential for distortion here because of my own experience. In the
initial process of evaluating my five children, I
was asked to recall my prenatal conditioning. This
questionnaire included items such as diet, extended family history, and the ages during which
specific development took place in the lives of my

children from birth. My accuracy in recalling these facts regarding five pregnancies and births surely falters. (Where's the journal when you really need it?)

Unfortunately, the potential for personal perception to cause inaccurate diagnosis doesn't stop with caregivers. Teachers, psychologists, and medical professionals can have differences of opinion about what is "normal attention" and "deficit attention," or how much physical movement is interpreted as "hyperactive."

These are the types of problems that keep members of the medical community skeptical and critical concerning the condition. Even ADD proponents voice similar legitimate concerns, such as Michael Gordon, Ph.D., director of the attention deficit hyperactive disorder programs at the State University of New York Health Science Center: "Unless we reserve the A.D.D. label for the truly beleaguered, I'm afraid that we will end up trivializing the disorder by treating personality traits as mental illness."[4]

If there's so much uncertainty about ADD, then why is it so popular? Why has it been so widely accepted that organizations like CHADD (Children and Adults with Attention Deficit Disorder) and A.D.D.A. (Attention Deficit Disorder Association) have been formed and are growing at a rapid pace? The answer is fairly simple. Thousands of people are now identifying behavior problems and finding meaningful help through receiving this diagnosis. Many stories of those who have been helped are so incredibly dramatic it appears miraculous. Drs. Hallowell and Ratey relate story after story of changed lives in *Driven to Distraction*.

Thom Hartmann also shares the success stories of people who told him of their personal victories, via the ADD Forum on CompuServe in his book *ADD Success Stories*. A host of other publications recount major personal achievements as a result of being diagnosed as having ADD.

In our family, one such story is of our son Gannon, whose story I tell with his permission. Throughout his years of education in private schools, we were regularly told by teachers what a wonderful individual he was but that we should hold him back a grade because of his "emotional immaturity" and "inability to stay on task." We were always personally convinced of Gannon's intellectual ability but couldn't understand his weak academic performance at school. His grades were erratic: A's in subjects of interest and a seesaw of A's to F's in things that bored him, along with numerous checks on the self-control charts. At home he had trouble remembering chores and even personal tasks. Eventually, we had him go through a battery of academic tests at a Sylvan Learning Center. "He should be producing straight A's," was the comment of his test evaluator.

We proceeded to try every method we could find to help him: daily checking of his assignment pad by his teachers, a variety of after-school study plans, day runners, spankings, privilege suspensions, etc., all to little avail. He was the object of our prayers, our love, and our commitment to his personal success. Yet, even with the best of Christian parenting, these kind of symptoms, which can dramatically affect academic performance, gradually erode a child's self-image. It was a con-

stant challenge to strengthen his confidence in
the midst of daily failures.

Gannon's grandfather was a constant source
of encouragement. "Not to worry," he would tell
us. "I was just like him, and I made out just fine."
Gannon was given the nickname "little Alfred"
after his grandfather and took pride in being
compared to such a wonderful man who is a pillar
of success in our community and a legend in the
Louisiana oil business.

I embarked on this experience of ADD discovery prior to his entering the eighth grade and
quickly realized that Gannon's symptoms were
classic manifestations of ADD. After discussing it
at length with my husband, Gary, we decided to
pursue having him tested. From that point on,
every step we took on behalf of Gannon evidenced
the blessing of God. Out of the wide variety of
individuals in our city qualified to test for ADD,
God graciously connected us with a wonderful
Christian evaluator by the name of Cindy DeVall
of DeVall Counseling Services. After working up
our family profile, conducting interviews, and
completing a variety of tests with Gannon, she
concluded that he was indeed ADD and gave us
a list of medical doctors to choose from for his
follow-up work. Much to our delight, one of them
was a Christian pediatrician with whom I had personally spent time discussing child-rearing practices; and I set Gannon's appointment with him.

Our visit with Dr. Prather was uplifting. He
explained to us what I already had learned in my
studies, about the frontal areas of the brain not
receiving enough chemical stimulation to develop
the habits needed for our educational system, and

suggested that we try a few months of treatment with Ritalin. He felt that the temporary use of Ritalin would give Gannon the opportunity to see what it's like to be ordered and focused in his thoughts and that Gannon would be able to develop the new habits and patterns of thought necessary to function effectively in school. Dr. Prather told us that 50 percent of his patients treated with Ritalin only used it temporarily for the purpose of having an opportunity to retrain the brain. That encouraged us. The idea of retraining the brain implies that it's not an "illness" we're dealing with but a specific type of brain that doesn't function in a manner that serves the needs of our culture or easily fits into it. This was an important discovery, since it strengthened my belief that ADD was not as much a medical problem as a cultural problem. In time, this theory would be proved to us through Gannon's experience and a host of other cases with which we would become involved.

When I was picking up Gannon from school after his first day on Ritalin, I sat in the carpool line waiting anxiously to hear his report. "Well, how did you make out?" I nervously asked. "Mom, I had peace all day long. I was able to take my time on my math exam. I can't wait to see my grade." Within a matter of days, the teachers were calling to let me know what a dramatic change they had seen in Gannon's ability to perform academically, and he was bringing home A's and B's with a sense of relief and pride.

Dr. Prather had mentioned that we might try an occasional afternoon dose of Ritalin when studies were heavy for Gannon. This would enable him to see what it's like to study with a focused mind. One afternoon Gannon asked to try this in preparation for a big history exam. After an hour of going over and over his material, he approached me in the kitchen. "Hey Mom, guess what?" he said. "For the first time in my life, I'm really enjoying studying!"

He came home from school the next day, excited at how well the test went and dying to see the results. We were excited for him when he got an A on the exam. Even more astounding was the final A he received in history for his first nine weeks in eighth grade. It was encouraging to see how proud he was of his achievement. He had never gotten above a C in history or social studies on his report card. In addition to that, it was the first time ever that he didn't have any checks in the "behavior" column of his report card. Another first was his being selected as the school recipient for the Christian Character Award.

It was only a few weeks into the treatment that Gannon came home from school and told me, "Today I forgot to take my noon dose at school, and I was able to concentrate all afternoon long. I think I'm figuring out how to concentrate." I called the school office and told the secretary to allow Gannon the freedom to take lower doses at noon or none at all, much to her surprise. As we've progressed along, Gannon has gradually been taking less and less Ritalin on his own initiative, maintaining his new grades, improving them in other subjects, and practicing new study habits.

I want to mention here that I don't believe Gannon should have had to take Ritalin at all. Our educational system is not setup for the broad variety of individual learning styles with which our children present them, particularly the visual learner like Gannon. Yet, I believe that will be changing as more and more parents confront our senior educators with the reality that black and white textbook learning shouldn't dominate our educational system. An integration of other methods, which include more visual learning and physical activity, would be of benefit to all students. Until we get to that place, it's a relief to know that there is help for the visual learner. Likewise, our culture, which is highly structured, time-oriented, and methodical, clashes with the type of brain that is free-spirited, spontaneous, and seeks stimulation.

I don't want to close out this initial chapter about ADD without touching on the subject of adults with ADD. When I began my journey into this field, before even dealing with my children, I first realized that I am an adult who has ADD. While reading *Driven to Distraction*, I recognized that I had been plagued by the symptoms of the condition as a child. In their book, Drs. Hallowell and Ratey developed diagnostic criteria for adults, which I'd like to share with you.[5]

NOTE: Consider a criterion met only if the behavior is considerably more frequent than that of most people of the same mental age.

A. A chronic disturbance in which at least twelve of the following are present:

    1. A sense of underachievement, of not meeting one's goals (regardless of how much one has actually accomplished).

    2. Difficulty getting organized.

3. Chronic procrastination or trouble getting started.

4. Many projects going simultaneously; trouble with follow-through.

5. A tendency to say what comes to mind without necessarily considering the timing or appropriateness of the remark.

6. A frequent search for high stimulation.

7. An intolerance for boredom.

8. Easy distractibility, trouble focusing attention, tendency to tune out or drift away in the middle of a page or a conversation, often coupled with the ability to hyperfocus at times.

9. Often creative, intuitive, highly intelligent.

10. Trouble in going through established channels, following "proper" procedure.

11. Impatient; low tolerance of frustration.

12. Impulsive, either verbally or in action, as in impulsive spending of money, changing plans, enacting new schemes or career plans, and the like; hot-tempered.

13. A tendency to worry needlessly, endlessly; a tendency to scan the horizon looking for something to worry about, alternating with inattention to or disregard for actual dangers.

14. A sense of insecurity.

15. Mood swings, mood lability, especially when disengaged from a person or project.

16. Physical or cognitive restlessness.

17. A tendency toward addictive behavior.

18. Chronic problems with self-esteem.

19. Inaccurate self-observation.

20. Family history of ADD or manic-depressive illness or depression or substance abuse or other disorders of impulse control or mood.

B. Childhood history of ADD. (It may not have been formally diagnosed, but in reviewing the history, one sees that the signs and symptoms were there.)

C. Situation not explained by other medical or psychiatric condition.

Within the chapter in which this list appears, "How Do I Know If I Have It?" the authors state the following:

> Whatever diagnostic criteria one refers to, it cannot be stressed too firmly how important it is not to diagnose oneself. While the information and examples presented here may lead you to suspect that you or your child or a relative has ADD, an evaluation by a physician to confirm the diagnosis and to rule out other conditions is essential.[6]

For those who want to pursue receiving medical treatment of the condition, these statements are paramount. As I will explain later in this book, "ruling out other conditions" is truly the starting point when looking into these behavior problems. Yet, I also believe that many of the adult Christians who will look into this condition for themselves will find, like myself, that a medical diagnosis isn't necessary in order to gain some very helpful personal insights. These insights can provide the opportunity to resolve problems and bring closure to issues that have been an annoyance to individuals throughout their spiritual pilgrimage.

Dr. John Ratey poignantly expresses the positive effects of recognizing ADD in one's life. The following was taken from Dr. Ratey's foreword to Thom Hartmann's book *ADD Success Stories*. With his permission, I've condensed his thoughts as follows:

> ADD is very much a nonlinear condition that does not have clear boundaries and sharp delineations. It displays a spectrum of variations, presenting symptoms from a mild impairment to a mild to moderate disability to a virtual handicap that, for some, makes it impossible to function in the world. ADD is a neurologic syndrome expressed in a number of different brain regions that varies in presentation in almost everyone who has the diagnosis. The condition itself changes in different contexts over time and an individual's environment has a considerable effect on the condition. Taking cues from the nature versus nurture debate, there are those who believe ADD is entirely biological and consequently beyond treatment, and others who believe environmental adjustments can reduce the deficits, enhance the assets, and provide a better life beyond that of predetermined genetic destiny. ADD is a prime example of a spectrum disorder that is biologically determined, yet is often best treated by environmental manipulation through what we call environmental engi-

neering. The treatment often involves setting up an environment in which it is possible to win rather than lose. As people are
diagnosed with this condition, and granted
permission to be who they are, it compels
them to reach previously unattempted
heights. When the shackles of shame are
lifted, the future can be approached with a
cleaner, crisper, more energetic viewpoint.[7]

I can honestly say that I'm approaching life
from a cleaner, crisper, more energetic viewpoint
since learning about ADD, making adjustments in
my thoughts and relationships based on the things
I've come to understand about myself.

As I was reflecting on the criteria suggested
for evaluating adults, it became clear to me that
my many years of appropriating the truths of the
Bible to my life had enabled me to overcome many
of the symptoms listed in the criteria. For example, having learned the value of times of rest,
meditation, and reflection in Christ, I was able to
overcome the intolerance for boredom and need
for high-stimulation activities. Those traits had
driven my childhood years (and driven my mother
crazy!). In becoming convinced of the importance
to trust God in all situations, I overcame much of
my tendency to worry about anything and everything. My desire to become like Christ in character had helped me to develop patience, self-control, and a desire to follow-through on my commitments, which had all been stumbling blocks in
my youth. In recognizing these things, I felt a
greater appreciation to God for the Bible and
how the study of it had given me victory over
symptoms that had been destructive in my life.

I also recognized that many of the symptoms typical to ADD were still an underlying problem in my life. They weren't controlling or ruining my life but were definitely producing a kind of "static" in my soul, interfering with my peace of mind and creating irritation in relationships. As I began to recognize these symptoms as part of the ADD package, I had renewed energy. I became enthusiastic about tackling these symptoms from a new approach. It would take me many pages to go over the list of twenty symptoms from the diagnostic criteria and share with you my experience, but I would like to share a few with you to illustrate the positive impact that the study of ADD has had on my life.

I'll begin with the first item on the list: A sense of underachievement, of not meeting one's goals (regardless of how much one has actually accomplished). No matter how hard I tried, I was incapable of having a sense of achievement in life. Intellectually I know that my life has been filled with many accomplishments, but I never sensed it in terms of feeling satisfied. This lack of satisfaction can cause us to pursue things in search of satisfaction. From a spiritual standpoint, Christians are to possess a sense of peace and satisfaction in the simple daily tasks of life. We are told that "whatever you do, whether in word or deed, do it all in the name of the Lord Jesus, giving thanks to God the Father through him" (Col. 3:17). Christ is to fill the void in our lives, and part of that void is our sense of satisfaction, of living life with purpose. Because I had a gnawing lack of this, I felt shame and guilt, like something was wrong with my faith. I knew it didn't have anything to do with my acceptance by God because I've always been convinced of His great love, but I felt that somehow I wasn't receiving or appropriating that reality. As a result of that, there was always a shadow, a question in my mind about what I was doing. If God was behind my actions, then I should feel satisfied, or at least somewhat fulfilled when I accomplished things through service to others, but I didn't.

This problem fueled another problem, which is criteria number eighteen: chronic problems with self-esteem. A lack of the sense of completion can lead to feelings of worthlessness, which has also gnawed at me on and off over the years. I have always known what the Bible says about me (beloved of God, His treasure) and I have had countless people give me praise, encouragement, and gratitude, for who I am and what I do in Christ. In fact, I have kept a file labeled "encouragement," which holds the loving letters of people over the years who have thanked me and encouraged me along the way. When I would get stuck in depression and frustration, I would pull them out and read them to help me refocus on my purpose. My husband has been my biggest fan and friend, and yet I have chronically suffered with poor self-esteem.

I realized that this was also connected to my having criteria symptom number nineteen: inaccurate self-observation. Over the years there have been many times when my husband would explain to me that I wasn't seeing myself—communication, attitudes, behaviors—clearly but was inaccurate in my self-perception, and I knew he was right, which added more guilt, shame, and frustration. My mind would see things about myself along a very narrow track, and I would suddenly come to realize how limited my view had been despite my efforts to have seen the whole picture. This pattern of experience can be quite discouraging.

In the study of ADD, I learned that these symptoms are often the result of the inability of the frontal lobes to sort out, categorize, and connect events and experiences, causing life to be a series of events that just melt together. This inhibits one's ability to perceive consequences, profit from past experience, and "connect the dots" of life, so to speak. For someone in another culture and another time, that might not interfere whatsoever in the function of one's life. However, in our society, structure, categorizing, connecting the dots, and coordinating the events of life are essential to feeling a part of the "normal" sector of our culture.

I am reminded of all the times that I made repeated mistakes in situations and felt great frustration because I could never seem to learn from past experience. I often felt embarrassment and shame about this. Once I understood and observed the differences in my brain patterns and the natural tendency to let thoughts race without developing structure, I understood it wasn't an issue of personal failings. I came into a new liberty, a new sense of well-being, and had an immediate release of guilt, shame, condemnation, and frustration. Besides that, I experienced a new power over my thought patterns, learning to quickly recognize incorrect or incomplete thoughts and dismiss them readily, no longer wrestling with them as some piece of a jigsaw puzzle in my soul that didn't fit. I have enjoyed more personal satisfaction after my discovery of ADD than I had in forty years of life. It has given me insight into certain traits that are at the core of who I am. I have truly been delivered of the crippling aspect of this condition and entered into a time of enhancing the assets, which I will share later in this book.

Beyond all this, I am blessed in becoming sensitive to these thought patterns in my children and am now able to teach them to be overcomers in their personal lives. I have learned, and am convinced, that in gleaning truths from the ADD community, many Christians will be empowered to take responsibility for behaviors that have been a stumbling block in their lives. This can serve to free them from elements of guilt, fear, and disappointment that have overshadowed their experience in Christ.

> For I know the plans I have for you, declares the Lord, plans to prosper you and not to harm you, plans to give you hope and a future. Then you will call upon me and come and pray to me, and I will listen to you. You will seek me and find me when you seek me with all your heart. (Jer. 29:11-13)

2. The Root Cause: A Biblical View

For everything that was written in the past was written to teach us, so that through endurance and the encouragement of the Scriptures we might have hope.
— Romans 15:4

One of the first hurdles people have to leap over in looking into attention deficit disorder is the word *disorder*. It is really disconcerting for people to think of their personal condition, or that of their children, as being a disorder. I have been amazed at the response of Christians when I mention that I believe many people are grappling with the symptoms of this condition. I've seen responses of anger, repulsion, resentment, and fear, and have thought, "Boy, did I hit a nerve!" I realize some of these reactions are because "disorders" in the medical community carry a stigma with them, and no one wants to carry a label that makes them seem less than normal— whatever normal is. (Another chapter will deal more in-depth with the disorder issue.)

In the Christian community there is also the
tendency of people to think Jesus, or religious
activity, is the only solution to life's problems.
Historically, the Church has resisted looking to
the sciences for possible answers to problems. It
was feared that such knowledge would become a
"substitute religion" for people, and in many cases
it did just that. This has created a tension between
the two disciplines of science and religion that
reaches back for centuries, at times being very
hostile towards one another. However, I have to
agree with Sir Isaac Newton's approach, which
was presented to me in the book *Integration
Musings: Thoughts on Being a Christian Professional*
by Dr. H. Newton Maloney of Fuller Theological
Seminary. In his book he states:

> Newton marveled at the intricacy of nature
> and contended that the human eye, for ex-
> ample, could never have come into being
> without a master designer with supernatu-
> ral power. Newton reasoned from nature
> to nature's God. For him, science and faith
> were one and the same. He helped write
> the preamble for the Royal Society of Sci-
> ence which dedicated the society to "dis-
> covering the truths of God and the allevia-
> tion of human suffering."
>
> . . . "All truth is God's truth," Newton would
> assert. The laws of human functioning are
> the laws of God.[1]

A member of our congregation just recently
came to the podium to give glory to God concerning this very idea. His thirteen-year-old daughter
had an extreme scoliosis of the spine and had
come to church that day, only twelve days after

major back surgery, having been the object of our fervent prayers. His testimony went like this:

> I want to thank God for revealing to the medical world new technology to correct physical deformities. Just a few years ago, doctors wouldn't have been able to help my daughter. There was no treatment for the severity of her condition. Now, through new technology, which I know only God could have revealed to the medical doctors, they were able to correct her spine. In addition to that, she walked into church today only twelve days after surgery. That is a miracle itself that shows God's great power and mercy, and I give Him the praise for it.

I know all of us would prefer miraculous healings and they certainly continue to occur, but God also deserves credit for the healing we receive through what knowledge He reveals to mankind in the sciences.

When I was in the middle of researching ADD, I just happened to also be in the middle of teaching a four-week, in-depth Bible study. It was about the condition of mankind from Creation to the present, and on to the final state of redemption at Christ's return. Whatever spiritual concerns I had about this condition were being answered in the lessons I was teaching, and I was fascinated with the correlation of the two studies. I'd like to share some of those findings with you.

The first lesson of the study that I was teaching was on the state of man in the Garden of Eden. It surveyed the advent of sin and how it created a tremendous disorder that affected the whole of creation. I realized that every disorder present today, whether in the sciences or humanities, is a direct result of the effect of sin on the universe. Consider some of the facts from the Bible's first book, Genesis, with me.

When God created our world, all that He created was an expression of His nature. All the laws of the universe, physical and natural, were in perfect harmony with His divine essence. Man was created in complete spiritual harmony, in a state of "perfection" that was consistent with God's being. He conducted his life from a heart centered on the fulfillment of God's will, naturally yielding to the laws of God which governed the creation.

Then enters the serpent who tells Eve that mankind would "be like God" if they would act independent of God's command and eat the forbidden fruit. Upon eating the fruit, mankind exchanged a God-centered heart for one of self-centeredness, altering the original state dramatically. God Himself declared the change, saying to the woman, "I will greatly increase your pains in childbearing; with pain you will give birth to children. Your desire will be for your husband and he will rule over you," and to the man,

> Cursed is the ground because of you;
> through painful toil you will eat of it all the
> days of your life. It will produce thorns and
> thistles for you, and you will eat the plants
> of the field. By the sweat of your brow you
> will eat your food until you return to the
> ground, since from it you were taken; for
> dust you are and to dust you will return.
> (Gen. 3:16-19)

Pain, suffering, and a clear departure from the perfection of God's original creation encompassed the earth.

Where man was once dominated by the pure essence of God, he is now dominated by a self-centered heart, subject to the laws of sin. As God clearly points out, man's physical body departed from the laws of divine health. Healthy organic action was no longer in perfection but was grossly affected, impaired by the laws of physical death, and a gradual erosion of God's perfect creation was set in motion. Since that time, human life has degenerated from Adam's life span of 930 years to a mere average of 80 years. Sickness and disease have progressed along their evil path, mutating, degenerating, and challenging man's ability to keep himself alive. All of nature revolves around the cycle of death itself. The truth is, all of mankind is in a state of disorder, not just those of us with ADD.

Moving on in the Bible study, we looked at man's inability to change his condition. We studied God's plan to release man from the bonds of hopelessness by sending His own Son, Jesus Christ, to make atonement for all the sins of mankind. This was our second lesson, entitled "The Regenerated Man." We learned that when a man accepts the sacrifice of God's Son, the Holy Spirit performs an act of "regeneration" or "rebirth," creating a new heart within him. This new heart has been "created in righteousness and true holiness" (Eph. 4:24), restoring to man a heart that recognizes God's will as preeminent.

We also learned that the completion of man's redemption—body, soul, and spirit—does not take place until Christ's return.

> The creation waits in eager expectation for the sons of God to be revealed. For the creation was subjected to frustration, not by its own choice, but by the will of the one who subjected it, in hope that the creation itself will be liberated from its bondage to decay and brought into the glorious freedom of the children of God. We know that the whole creation has been groaning as in the pains of childbirth right up to the present time. Not only so, but we ourselves, who have the firstfruits of the Spirit, groan inwardly as we wait eagerly for our adoption as sons, the redemption of our bodies. (Rom. 8:19-23)

This suggests that, as Christians, we continue to struggle with the weakened physical state produced by Adam's sin. The idea of ADD stemming from a biological weakness is clearly within the realm of possibility for the Christian mindset.

The study continued. We considered the good news for our bodies in this life. As Christians, we experience degrees of revival, renewal, and even miraculous healings—"foretastes" of that perfection which is to come. Our souls experience greater and greater degrees of the glory and presence of God, changing our character into Christ's likeness, as we "put on" the new nature within us.

From here, I began studying the Scriptures concerning our human frailty and came across the many Scriptures of the New Testament that refer to our continued state of weakness. The Apostle Paul often reminds us of our human limitations and of our complete dependence on God. In many of the Epistles, it's made clear to us that physically, outwardly, we are in a state of perishing (2 Cor. 4:16), with an ongoing potential for natural body system failures. I recalled the many loving Christian friends I've lost to cancer, including both of my parents. I thought about my many dear friends, faithful to the Cross, who struggle with infirmities in the form of diabetes, failing eyesight, heart attacks, colitis, migraines, and arthritis—just to name a few.

As I thought about brain disorders, my heart went out to Evangelist Billy Graham and his family, facing his struggle with the debilitating Parkinson's disease. I realized that Christians who are sickly and most in need of support are often faced with ambivalence, legalistic attitudes, or awkward avoidance by the Christian community. Too many Christians turn to "blame" and "avoidance," rather than "empathy" and "compassion" when dealing with sickness in others. This is especially true of illnesses related to the mind. Some brain disorders such as strokes, Alzheimer's, and Parkinson's disease, are generally accepted as normal maladies of the brain especially in old age. Yet, there is a lot of resistance to disorders of brain function in conditions such as mental illness, manic depression, schizophrenia, and the neurotransmitter problems thought to be associated with ADD. After studying the cause of this resistance, I concluded that it was related to the fact that these disorders affect a person's behavior.

For Christians, behavior problems are generally believed to be the direct result of willful moral failure. The reason for this is probably rooted in the earlier mentioned reality of the "new nature" within us, which includes the presence of God's Holy Spirit. We are told that if we live by the Spirit, we will not gratify the desires of the sinful nature (Gal. 5:16). We are encouraged to live according to the fruits of the Spirit, which are listed in Galatians 5:22-23: "love, joy, peace, patience, kindness, goodness, faithfulness, gentleness, and self-control." These "fruits" are directly related to behaviors, so it is natural to assume that those who aren't producing them are in some way personally failing to put on the new nature, or are irresponsible in their walk with God. Although all of these assumptions might be valid, they don't take into consideration the potential for a failure in the function of the brain system as a cause of behavior problems. Christian psychologists will tell you, it is more than a possibility; for many, it is a scientific reality!

As I delved into the study of Christian behavior problems, I began to examine what our approach should be in dealing with them. After all, most of the people reading this book are doing so because they are dealing with behaviors, in themselves or their children, that do not conform to what the Christian Church, educational system, or American society consider "normal," or healthy. As a children's ministry director, I have faced these issues repeatedly over the years while assisting parents with child-rearing concerns, and would like to share with you what I believe the Bible tells us our approach in these matters should be.

First, and foremost, every concern and difficulty we face in life should be brought before the Lord in prayer. I realize this might sound simplistic, but in twenty years of ministry, I have found that one of the greatest things lacking in people's approach to problems is fervent prayer. I've had innumerable occasions in which a distressed parent has told me about a child's behavior and their inability to get a handle on it. Nine times out of ten, there has been a very low commitment to prayer in the situation. This fact has always distressed me in dealing with parents, because they have overlooked the most powerful force a Christian has at his disposal. Too often, people want a quick fix to the behavior problems of their children, but haven't even made a commitment in prayer to receive help from God on the matter.

We should never underestimate the power of prayer, but frequently do. Incredible miracles take place in the human body as a direct result of prayer and our loving Father's compassionate response to it. I have been present to witness tumors shrink, crippled people walk, deaf ears open, and have even known minds that have been healed from years of drug abuse. I have witnessed the lives of individuals who had damaged their brains from years of drug and alcohol abuse restore their brains through prayer and are now able to live successful, healthy lives. Even the media is reporting on doctors who claim that praying people recover quicker than those who don't. They claim that their patients who have exercised deep religious convictions recover much quicker than those who were without religious faith.

It's important that we continue to pray even when we don't receive immediate healing. The Scriptures clearly tell us that persistent prayer produces results. One encouraging reference is in the Book of James: "The prayer of a righteous man is powerful and effective. Elijah was a man just like us. He prayed earnestly that it would not rain, and it did not rain on the land for three and a half years. Again he prayed, and the heavens gave rain, and the earth produced its crops" (5:16-18).

So it is crucial that we approach any concerns we have concerning our children's behavior, our own behavior, and the behavior of those we love, with fervent, consistent prayers of faith. In practical terms this means having a time of daily prayer before God, pouring out your concerns and asking for His help and guidance. Depending on how serious you are about it, fasting is a good expression of prayer as well. As a matter of fact, if you skip a meal you would have an entire hour to spend with the Lord in supplication. Even if the symptoms are small, bring them to God in prayer, before they grow large.

Another important biblical factor in facing behavioral problems is the need to be people of discernment. To be "dull" comes quite naturally to us as humans, but we are told to be people who are "watchful" and "alert" in all things (Col. 4:2, 1 Thess. 5:6). God has provided us with the means to do so by the presence of His Holy Spirit within us. Along with that, we are encouraged to ask God for "wisdom" who gives "generously to all without finding fault" (James 1:5). Discernment is something that must be "exercised" (Heb. 5:14). We must look at things beyond their surface value. Jesus was a man of discernment of whom it was prophesied, "He will not judge by what he sees with his eyes, or decide by what he hears with his ears" (Isa. 11:3). We often read of Him detecting what the truth was beyond the exterior appearance.

I like Dr. Newton Maloney's definition of discernment in another section of his book *Integration Musings*. He says it is the "penetrating analysis of the dimensions of the situation" and an "appreciation for the several layers of meaning in a given event."[2] An important inference here is that behaviors are complex in nature and are frequently a mere symptom of a deeper issue.

What we perceive as negative behaviors are often positive signs in that they are indicators to us of something gone awry. For instance, anger is our soul's way of warning us that something has gone wrong in a situation, and pains in our body—though discomforting—are often there to warn us of a deeper problem in our body's system that needs our attention. Unfortunately, most people don't give much attention to these signals, looking at them from the surface. They are seen as a normal "part of life," rather than being seen as indicators.

It is common for people to deal with their symptoms through denial, or to eliminate them through the use of medications. This can give them a false sense of well-being, while underneath the problems are still there. Life goes on as usual, while an underlying problem may be brewing. It is not uncommon for doctors to face a scenario such as receiving a new patient who has taken an antacid for stomach discomfort for years, who finally gets checked out only to discover cancer in the stomach that could have easily been resolved if it had been addressed in the early stages.

This is equally true of behaviors. When left unchecked, they can develop into serious problems. Children, from their earliest days, display behaviors that act as "indicators" to alert the discerning parent that something needs their attention. Parents of newborns are especially "discerning" people, acutely aware of their babies needs. What is making the baby cry? Is it a wet diaper, hunger, fear, insecurity, or loud noise? It seems that parents begin child rearing with a discerning heart but somehow lose that edge as the children grow in their ability to care for themselves. Perhaps that's because it takes so much energy to stay on that edge of being watchful and alert. Believe me, I know how much energy it takes. I have five children to oversee, and it can be quite overwhelming at times. They are each going through different stages of life simultaneously. Remaining alert to their personal needs is a constant challenge.

Unfortunately, as children grow, parents often begin to dismiss their behaviors as simple "child's play" or "common to life." A little girl cries for no apparent reason and is told to "be quiet"; a young boy begins lashing out at siblings and is told to "just stop it"—neither being given the time nor energy necessary to get to the root of the problem. Too often, a child receives parental involvement only when a particular symptom makes life uncomfortable for the parent, rather than as a result of being particularly sensitive to the child.

We need to become people who look beyond the exterior. This is of utmost importance in dealing with the behavior symptoms of ADD. As I will explain more fully later in this book, there are a host of reasons for these behaviors besides the possibility of a biological mishap. It takes a discerning heart and hard work to sort through the "dimensions of a situation" and understand the "several layers of meaning in an event," but we have been equipped to do so; it is a matter of priority.

Another biblical factor to consider in our approach to problems is the common practice of applying the Scriptures as a means to overcome difficulties. This is practiced in many forms, such as meditating on certain verses that apply to a particular situation, reminding God in prayer of biblical promises, and even audibly quoting verses in faith. These valid practices, which we are encouraged to do in the Bible, can produce striking results. Yet there is an additional approach frequently overlooked and even shunned at times in the Christian community—the study of natural causes, in this case, the human condition. I made a similar reference to this when mentioning Sir Isaac Newton's belief that "all truth is God's truth." He believed we should seek out scientific truth which could lead us to the understanding needed in addressing difficulties. Time and experience have taught us that, although there are times when the spoken word has an immediate affect, there are also times when understanding of our condition provides solutions. Be it physical, mental, emotional, or spiritual, knowledge about our condition can be a conduit for the Word to have its powerful effect and bring change into our lives.

In practical terms, Jesus used that which is natural to make a spiritual impact on His disciples. Surely He, being God in the flesh, could have simply spoken "the word" and miraculously affected their intellectual understanding. Instead, He chose to appeal to their natural understand-

ing as a means to bring about change in their
hearts and minds, using illustrations from nature
and natural life situations to impact their lives
(i.e., lilies of the field, weather elements, illustra-
tive parables, etc.). We also have Paul telling Timothy to use a little wine for his stomach problems
and many infirmities in 1 Timothy 5:23—looking
to the treatments and technology of that era to
resolve Timothy's ailments.

We can all greatly benefit from the new light
being shed on natural functions and causations,
which can reveal the natural core of a matter in
order to alleviate human suffering. There is no
question that theology excels worldly knowledge
because it holds the keys to eternal life, but we
cannot dismiss the natural resources of intellect
and inspiration which God has provided all mankind with. Jesus utilized them, using them as
pathways for the light of God to give understanding, and we can greatly benefit by the use of them
as well.

In looking, then, into the Bible, what can we
see about ADD? I believe we can see that God
created mankind as a gifted creature which repro-
duces uniquely gifted individuals, born with inherent traits designed to serve a specific purpose.
Natural giftings and abilities have been hampered
and distorted because of the disorder set into the
creation with the advent of sin. This has created
difficulties in every area of life. The brain is a
conduit for the expression of our talents and gifts.
It, too, has been impacted by the damaging affect
of sin on the whole of creation and can act out of
balance. In some cases, the weakened condition
of the brain can become injurious to the indi-

vidual. Our attitude toward people who experience these difficulties should be compassion, encouragement, and support. A spiritual response includes prayer, discernment, Bible study, and a study of the natural information available in our day and age.

We are not yet experiencing the full redemption purchased for us on the Cross but are in a gradual process of experiencing new life. We look forward with hope to a day in the future when God will arrest every disorder in the universe caused by the effects of sin. On that day, He will bring to completion the work for which Christ suffered and died: the redemption of all things.

> Being confident of this, that he who began
> a good work in you will carry it on to
> completion until the day of Christ Jesus.
> (Phil. 1:6)

3. Lemons to Lemonade

And we know that in all things God works for the good of those who love him, who have been called according to His purpose.

—Romans 8:28

Arrayed in animal skins with the appearance of a native American, Nobatchu sat crouched low in the thick forest of western Canada. The crisp scent of the forest air filled his senses, stirring anticipation of the meal he was about to capture for his village. His eyes darted wildly across the terrain from the rustle of foliage fifty yards behind his left shoulder, over to the screeching hawk passing across the horizon toward the right of his hidden location, and back across the forest to the distant sound of snow being downtrodden by a mysterious forest creature. A million hunts raced through his mind, his thoughts navigating information in search of similarities: the season, the wind, the placement of sunlight, the sounds, the smells, all revealing the possibilities that this day's hunt could bring. The next breeze came from the north carrying with it the familiar scent of a deer. Nobatchu silently turned to look northward; his hunting impulse reawakened by the sight of approaching deer on the outlying hills. Another scan of memories set into place what action he must and must not take to be rewarded with the taste of venison on the lips of all his kin.

I wrote the above paragraph in order to demonstrate the lemonade produced by such lemons as impulsivity, distractibility, restlessness, and hyperactivity. Nobatchu would be called ADD if placed in a Western workplace. He probably would be medicated with Ritalin for his overly attentive mind and with Zoloft for the subsequent depression he'd encounter trying to function within the confines of a typical place of business. Yet if he was schooled in understanding his biological make-up, he could do quite well as a fitness trainer, cinematographer, sound effects technician, or fighter pilot and would probably live a fruitful life.

Clearly, when these traits are recognized as positives, they can be harnessed and utilized, becoming a true asset in the life of a person we now call ADD. This process can begin by reversing the negative view of the symptoms of ADD and interpreting them from a positive lens. If I had the opportunity to perform ADD evaluations as a professional, I would hope to introduce the positive side of the symptoms in a manner that would uplift the individual. More than anything, I believe they need hope, faith in God, and restored self-esteem. My desire would be to empower children and adults to pursue change. Following is my example of how I might go about doing this. I will speak in the first person as if directly speaking to a child or adult with ADD, addressing the symptoms in the DSM-IV as listed in the first chapter:

You have a tremendous amount of energy inside of you; the kind of energy that helped Benjamin Franklin discover electricity in the storm, and helped Thomas Edison convert it into a light bulb. Use that energy to learn more about the things that are of interest to you. If you will seek to capture that energy and use it for doing constructive things, there will be no limit to what God can accomplish through your life.

God has given you the kind of body that has the ability to be very active, which means you need to get a lot of exercise. This can make it difficult for you to sit still for long periods of time. It is important that you make an extra effort to do physical activities many times during the day. Whether you're at the stage in life where you can run endlessly at recess or climb stairs at work, make time to use your energy. This will make it easier for you to sit still when you must. Stay tuned in to your body's condition, and if you find yourself physically restless, find a way to get physically active or at least make plans to do so. Get outdoors and run freely, allowing the physical energy you have to flow. God gave it to you, be sure to use it! You'd probably be great in sports—try them out!

Your mind is able to pay attention to so many things at one time that it's incredible. This can cause you a problem because so many things in modern life need our undivided attention. It's much easier for you to hop from one thing to another in your mind. The good news is that you also have the ability to get powerfully focused when you want to be, like when playing a video game, reading a book, or watching a favorite show. Be aware of your mind's tendency to think of many things at once. When you're in a situation in which you must stay focused, try to gather all of your energy as if playing a video game. Look steadily with your eyes and hyperfocus on the matter at hand.

In your free time let your thoughts run free, inviting God to use this gift to inspire you, teach you, and give you new ideas. You'll be amazed at how many things you can think of when looking at one simple object, hopping from thought to thought. Many inventions were created by people who think like you. With ideas always running through your mind, sometimes they can keep you from falling asleep at night. Be sure to do things before bedtime that relax you like reading or listening to relaxing music.

Being so full of thoughts makes it easy for you to talk to people. You always have something to talk about! Your many ideas can be very helpful to people, giving them new things to consider. On the other hand, it's also easy for you to talk too much and forget to give other people a chance to speak. Your mouth kind of acts like part of your brain. Sometimes those thoughts can be so loud in your mind that you don't even hear when other people are speaking. You must learn to practice when to speak and when to be silent. It can be like a game for you—a real challenge—but if anyone can win at this game, you can! Then again, you might be the quiet type who rarely speaks because you can't seem to catch your thoughts in time to speak them out. Your thoughts are very important, so make an effort to share them with others.

Those thoughts of yours can fly faster than a speeding bullet, which helps you to get many things done in a short amount of time. Also, it can cause you to be forgetful of what needs to be done or what you should or shouldn't do, which can make you feel bad about yourself. Look on the bright side and become a person who leaves clues, notes, and memos of what needs to be done. Find fun ways to do this: hang them, paste them, scribble them, color them, or just leave a trail, but develop a pattern of leaving reminders to help you stay aware of what needs to be done. At times when you forget, just remember it's because your mind is like a rapidly moving machine that overlooks things at times, and that's okay. There will always be another opportunity to remember what to do.

Getting things done right away is a gift you have that can be very useful. The way you think helps you get things done very quickly. Many people aren't like this, though, and need to have time to figure things out. In fact, many things (like growing food or building a house) require time, and if you rush them, there will be bad results. Because you can act quickly, at times you'll feel impatient and frustrated because things aren't moving along. When impatience flares, remind yourself that your way of doing things is not the only way and, in some situations, not the best way. Your mind is like a galloping horse and you must learn when to pull back the reins in your mind, and when to run full speed ahead and accomplish things fast. It's a lot of fun when you figure out the right time to move quickly and get things done in an amazing way. The important thing is to practice, practice, and practice until those reins work at your command!

ADD can be approached through enhancing the positive and learning to manage the negative. Instead of calling these people impulsive, which is commonly seen as a negative word, we should call them spontaneous; instead of hyperactive, we should call them energetic; instead of distractible, call them observant or vigilant. These positive words validate an individual's worth, giving them hope that they have God-given abilities that are meaningful and valuable in spite of chronic failures.

Lives can be changed from tragedy to triumph by taking steps to subvert the frustration suffered by people like Vincent Van Gogh and Hans Christian Anderson, who experienced great rejection because of their unusual behaviors. We can provide these kinds of people with an appreciation of who God created them to be. We have the understanding to help them overcome the persecution they experience from those who feel they are "abnormal," be it teachers, peers, or parents.

I continue to be "bothered" by the sour presentation of this type of individual by the term *Attention Deficit Disorder*, especially because I have come to learn how much it bothers others. For now it's what we're stuck with, and I'm working on getting over it. I hope you are too, because if you're this kind of person, then living your life being misunderstood, frustrated, and made fun of for your behavior is much worse than receiving the label of being ADD. Until a more sensible term is presented, I'm going to keep squeezing the lemon out of ADD and turning it into lemonade through majoring on the positive side of the common traits of the condition. I'll continue learning and sharing what practices can be employed to lessen the negative side of those symptoms.

What I'm really talking about is known as a paradigm shift. Originally, the word *paradigm* came from the Greek and was a scientific term. Today, it is commonly used to describe a frame of reference, theory, or model such as the "hunter and farmer" example discussed in the next chapter. The term is often used concerning our mind's understanding, and interpretation of things. In his book *The 7 Habits of Highly Effective People*, author Stephen R. Covey specifically addresses the fact that we have these paradigms or frames of reference in our minds, which dictate our life experiences. He calls them "maps":

> Each of us has many, many maps in our head, which can be divided into two main categories: maps of the way things are, or realities, and maps of the way things should be, or values. We interpret everything we experience through these mental maps. We seldom question their accuracy; we're usually even unaware that we have them. We simply assume that the way we see things is the way they really are or the way they should be. And our attitudes and behaviors

grow out of those assumptions. The way we
see things is the source of the way we think
and the way we act.[1]

Within this context, ADD is viewed as a "sour
lemon." It is seen as a disorder and a disability, or
as an excuse for unbridled behaviors. The belief
is that once you "have it," you're marked for life
as someone who is "problematic." What I'm attempting to do is give people information, understanding, and biblical insight to shift their paradigm concerning ADD into one that is likeable
and refreshing (i.e., lemonade). The difficulty in
doing this, as in changing any other paradigm, is
that it requires a changing of our old ways of
thinking, which often have become like concrete
"traditions" in our minds, and we know how hard
those are to break!

Resistance to changing ideas has been a problem for humanity since the beginning of time.
The American Civil War of the 1860s was fought
over such an issue. Slavery was a generational paradigm that was confronted with a new paradigm.
Each new scientific discovery has meant letting go
of former perceptions to embrace new ones. Consider how significantly our world view changed
when Copernicus revealed that the sun and not
the earth was at the center of the universe. Another quantum shift took place with the discovery
that the world is spherical instead of flat. The
people of that generation believed that the earth
was flat and were suddenly confronted with the
possibility that their perception was incomplete or
wrong.

Whether it is round or flat, it is still the planet
earth. In the same way, I'm not trying to chal-

lenge the essential premise of ADD being an issue of brain function. I'm endeavoring to point others to a deeper level of thinking about this condition.

Perceptions are a strange thing. In contemplating this, I was reminded of the current artwork known as 3D or Magic Eye, which is digitally generated by computer to hide a picture within a picture. My husband got into these before they were "cool." When he first brought it into the office one day, a group of us gathered to look at this picture of speckled color. He told us it was a three dimensional picture of dinosaurs, and we all laughed at him. I was the worst scorner, thinking he had really gone over the deep end.

After twenty minutes of staring at this thing until my eyes were watering, the dinosaurs suddenly popped out at me. I loudly exclaimed I'd seen it, almost shocked by the reality that there was something really there. I brought a print up to my sister's family in Oregon and excitedly told them of my gift. None of them could see the dinosaurs. They thought Gary and I had both gone nuts, but my sister agreed to hang it on the wall in hopes that someone would eventually see the scene I had been describing. It was several weeks later that she called to tell me her family had finally seen the dinosaurs. Now, 3D pictures are commonplace, because everyone has managed to shift how they look at the splash of color in hopes that their 3D fanatic friend was telling them the truth.

Although I've been talking about the need to change our vantage point concerning ADD, it's important to understand that it takes work. It's more than a change in thought; it also requires

action. We see this in the example of the Civil
War, where men fought not only to change the
idea of slavery, but to see slavery actually abol-
ished. Similarly, in the example of lemonade, it
takes work to make lemons into lemonade. Someone must squeeze the lemons, handle the empty
skins, which are acidic, deal with the sour tasting
liquid, and mix the right ingredients to make a
tasty refreshing drink. It's always easier to let a
lemon just be a lemon.

We all know the inspiring stories of people
who have turned their sour situations into experiences of victory. Joni Eareckson-Tada is one of
those inspiring people. As a young Christian, she
had a diving accident that made her a quadriple-
gic. In her book, *Joni,* she relates the story of her
difficulty adjusting to the reality that she would
never walk again and would have to live her life
dependent on others to do the simplest of things.

Out of a life of difficulty, she found grace to
overcome the depression and despair that were
hers. It required a lot of work (emotional squeezing, handling acidy thoughts, and tasting the bitterness of her situation) before she had the right
mixture to make her life one of refreshment and
blessing. She became a fantastic artist, using her
mouth to hold paintbrushes, creating paintings
most people can't produce with two hands! God
sent her a wonderful husband to meet her physical demands and emotional needs, and she's become a popular speaker on behalf of the handi-
capped. Her talks on radio about a relationship
with God are stirring.

There are many stories like this that inspire us
and speak to us of having courage in the midst of

our difficulties. Each of them point to the fact that it takes great effort and determination to turn situations that appear as sour lemons into situations that produce lemonade. For those who have only experienced the lemon side of ADD, I can assure you that lemonade can be produced, but it will take a concentrated effort. Once a person recognizes that they are an ADD type individual, they have to examine where they are being hindered by the negative side of the symptoms, decide on a plan to overcome it, and employ it. In this sense we understand that making a paradigm shift is just the beginning. It must be followed by action, which requires work, but the result is a beautiful picture in place of a handicap.

As for my story, from the onset I was hit with the negative perception people had of ADD. I was facing skepticism from the Christian community. Once educated, I became faced with the additional difficulty of explaining ADD to others. Somehow, by the grace of God, I saw how valuable knowledge about ADD could be, not only to myself but countless others. I saw the potential for lives to be liberated from past failures and patterns. Realizing this, I came to see the great potential for nurturing and educating children who would face great difficulty in the structure of our current society. Not only did I have a paradigm shift in my attitudes toward ADD, but I also determined to take action to employ it personally and then share it with others.

There is a purpose for the lemon hanging on the tree, and not just for lemonade but a host of other things. Likewise, each of us has a purpose. This purpose comes into view with each passing

year. Not many of us sense this plan early on in
life, but we watch it unfold year by year. We each
struggle to compensate for our weaknesses in the
hope that we will be able to perform that which
God designs for us. He knows the lemons that we
each have in our lives and He has the knowledge
to help us succeed. This fact should keep us willing to submit our weaknesses to God, asking for
help and then receiving it in whatever form it
comes to us, in order to become more effective as
His servant on this earth.

A monk once told Thom Hartmann back in
1978: "A person who is acting out of a grounded,
solid, real sense of who he is will have a force and
power to his actions that a person who's just doing things to get them done won't. He'll have a
more powerful and visible impact on the world."[2]

I'm for whatever it takes to fulfill the purpose
for which we have been created, learning to appreciate who we are as individuals, and growing
in our capacities. We all serve a God who wants
nothing more than to see us live productive lives.
"For we are God's workmanship, created in Christ
Jesus to do good works, which God prepared in
advance for us to do" (Eph. 2:10).

As Nobatchu walked with pounding steps
through the blanket of snow, he felt the warmth
of the freshly killed deer across his shoulders pen-
etrate through his winter covering. His thoughts
were filled with the memory of other kills, feasts,
and full stomachs. The sense of satisfaction gave
more energy to his stride as he crossed the ravine
on his final descent home. Hearing the voices of
the children crying out his name from a distance,
he lifted his head with pride to announce the gift

from God. The children began singing the familiar song of thanksgiving, encircling Nobatchu with
movement as he entered the village and laid down
his prey.

Once again preparations began for the sharing of food, and laughter passed among the tribe
as each performed their task while the scent of
roasting venison filled the air. Sitting in the noon-
day sun, they heartily ate their fill. Nobatchu's
eyes roamed the sea of faces, recalling the times
he'd failed them, coming back empty-handed
because he'd forgotten one detail or weapon or
moved too quickly, scaring off his prey. Those
days had become rare, he thought, for he'd learned
to refine his skillful ways, as his father had taught
him. He clutched the leather patch which hung
around his neck; a keepsake inscribed by his father and given to him after his first successful
hunt which read "well done, faithful son." He
raised it into the sunlight and bowed his head,
thanking God for the meal He'd provided this
day.

Each person is born with purpose, and each is
provided with the tools to accomplish it. Each of
us must find our way through the obstacles of life
with the help of God.

> Where can I go from your Spirit? Where
> can I flee from your presence? If I go up
> to the heavens, you are there; If I make my
> bed in the depths, you are there. If I rise
> on the wings of the dawn, if I settle on the
> far side of the sea, even there your hand
> will guide me, your right hand will hold
> me fast. If I say, Surely the darkness will
> hide me and the light become night around

me, even the darkness will not be dark to
you; the night will shine like the day, for
darkness is as light to you. For you created
my inmost being; you knit me together in
my mother's womb. I praise you because I
am fearfully and wonderfully made; your
works are wonderful, I know that full well.
My frame was not hidden from you when
I was made in the secret place. When I was
woven together in the depths of the earth,
your eyes saw my unformed body. All the
days ordained for me were written in your
book before one of them came to be. (Ps.
139:7-16)

4. A Gift from God

Every good and perfect gift is from above, coming down from the Father of lights, who does not change like shifting shadows.

—James 1:17

It sounds contradictory to call something labeled a "disorder" a "gift" from God, but the disorder aspect of this condition has to do with brain chemistry as opposed to behavior. Many of God's gifts within us are hampered by the frailty of our human condition. God's gifts to us, which He delivers in good and perfect condition, are commonly disrupted by the pervading corruption of our world. Fortunately, as with the disease of cancer, God is providing knowledge to help us treat the body disorders we struggle with as we remain in a corrupted environment until Christ's return. Consider what a gift the knowledge of antibiotics has been to alleviate physical suffering, even to the saving of lives. These kinds of gifts from God are truly good.

The use of the word *deficit* is also faulty and misleading. Dr. Hallowell makes reference to this in the preface of *Driven to Distraction*: "The syndrome is not one of attention deficit, but attention inconsistency; most of us with ADD can in fact hyperfocus at times."[1] Author Thom Hartmann also points to this in his book *ADD Success Stories*: "It's also often noted by ADD experts that it's not that ADDers can't pay attention to anything: it's that they pay attention to everything."[2] This has certainly been true in my experience. I have always had the ability to give my attention to a multitude of things at once and can keep track of many tasks simultaneously. This fact has always been a fascination to those around me. I'm sometimes perceived as a wonder woman and have always given God the glory for my ability to "do it all," knowing that apart from Him I can do nothing (John 15:5).

It came as a surprise to find myself in many pages of the various books on the subject of ADD. I would never have imagined that the study of this condition could inspire such deep personal insight, have practical value, and have a redemptive effect on talents. I found Thom Hartmann to be one of the most inspiring writers on the subject. His books are filled with many constructive ideas for improving the quality of life for people with ADD symptoms. He reverses the negative view of ADD characteristics from "symptoms" to "abilities," by directing our attention away from the "syndrome" focus to a more "gifted" focus. He has written several books on the subject, which I would recommend to anyone wanting to learn to

fix

capitalize on the assets and minimize the negatives of the condition. I was so encouraged in simply reading the introduction to his book *Attention Deficit Disorder: A Different Perception* that I would like to share these gleanings from it with you.

> Somewhere between six and twenty million men, women, and children in the United States suffer from attention deficit disorder or ADD. Millions more individuals possess many ADD-type characteristics even though they may have learned to cope so well that they don't think of themselves as people with attention-related problems. This book is the first I know of to present the idea that ADD is not always a disorder—but instead may be a trait of personality and metabolism; that ADD comes from a specific . . . need in the history of humankind; that ADD can actually be an advantage (depending on the circumstances); and that, through an understanding of the mechanism which led to ADD's presence in our gene pool, we can recreate our schools and workplaces to not only accommodate ADD individuals, but to allow them to again become the powers behind cultural, political, and scientific change which they have so often historically represented.[3]

In light of his referencing the historical portrayal of ADD-type individuals, I want to mention that many of the works I read named historical figures that are commonly thought to have had learning or behavior disorders. People such as Albert Einstein, Gen. George Patton, Hans Christian Andersen, Leonardo da Vinci, Benjamin

Franklin, Amadeus Mozart, and Thomas Edison were troubled by similar problems. Many of our historical heroes, such as these, suffered from a variety of the problems currently associated with ADD. They were scorned, rejected, and ridiculed because of their peculiarity, appearing "different" from the norm.

Thom Hartmann is very convincing in his approach to ADD, wanting to empower these types of people to capitalize on their brilliance to the benefit of us all. His books are thought-provoking, proposing a useful paradigm for people with ADD characteristics, which he calls the hunter and farmer model. In this comparison, he points out that the qualities found in ADD people are the same qualities prevalent in hunter-based civilizations. The distractibility, impulsivity, and risk-taking/restlessness attributed to ADD are qualities that are an asset in civilizations where hunting is the primary means of survival. Distractibility translates into a constant scanning of surroundings—a necessary survival skill for hunters. Impulsivity translates into the hunter's asset of making instant decisions without giving them a second thought, which is essential to successful hunting. The risk-taking/restlessness is what keeps hunters motivated and able to successfully provide for their families and communities. They view risk-taking as being a normal part of their daily existence.

Conversely, these same qualities have an adverse affect in our "farmer-like" society, particularly evidenced in the restricting structure of the educational system. The hunter's tremendous ability to "give attention to many things at once" translates into "distractibility" in the narrow confines of our school classrooms. Likewise the trait of "making quick decisions without thinking twice" translates into "impatience" and "impulsivity" in the highly controlled environments of our offices and schools. Finally, the "constant search for high stimulation" which helps keeps hunters interested in pursuing food, wreaks havoc for teachers, as well as in the personal lives of adults trying to function within the farmer-like confines of our society.

This hunter/farmer paradigm is a fascinating theory since it points to the fact that both the hunter and the farmer have different personality chemistries and giftedness that enables them to be productive in their own unique way. The hunter and the farmer both live productive lives. Each of them supply food for others, but accomplish it in different ways.

Perhaps it won't be long until Thom Hartmann's model of hunters and farmers becomes a common lens through which we all view ADD symptoms. I know I wouldn't mind being viewed as a hunter. Frankly, I could easily see myself out there in the forest with Nobatchu scanning the environment in my mind and through my senses, just waiting silently to make that one rapid lunge to capture dinner. Skinning an animal suddenly seems within the realm of possibility! Maybe we could start referring to it as BFV (Brain Function Variety) with a "dash" afterwards with the letter *H* for the hunter type and *F* for the farmer type, like BFV-H or BFV-F—just a thought!

A biblical basis for this concept is clearly laid out for us in 1 Corinthians 12 in which our differences are compared to the differing body parts, illustrating the importance and value of each unique part. These differences are attributed to God in verses 4-6: "There are different kinds of gifts, but the same Spirit. There are different kinds of service, but the same Lord. There are different kinds of working but the same God works all of them in all men."

Addressing personal issues in this way is not something new, but it is new to the ADD world. It is quite similar to the popular practice of examining personality traits through tests such as the Myers-Briggs test, Taylor-Johnson Temperament Analysis, and PDP Personality Survey. They can reveal one's strengths and weaknesses, helping people make life decisions and setting goals that will work for their individual chemistry. Christian writers, Gary Smalley and John Trent, seek to heal schisms in relationships caused by personality differences. Their book is entitled *The Two Sides of Love*. They liken the differing human personalities to the characteristics of animals, namely, the lion, beaver, otter, and golden retriever.[4] They express how certain personalities will typically irritate other types of personalities simply by their innate differences. Developing an understanding of personality variations will help us become more tolerant and sensitive to those who are unlike us.

Each of us can relate to the tension created by dealing with personalities opposite our own. Think of how often we find the neat person irritated with the messy person, or the calm person annoyed by the hyperactive type. Many punctual persons have been quite frustrated by the carefree individuals who pay little attention to time restraints.

Differences have always challenged mankind's ability to dwell in peace and harmony. Unfortunately, instead of appreciating differences and capitalizing on how they can complement other types of metabolisms, we commonly despise them. I have witnessed my share of spite toward the ADD community. It appears quite possible that ADD is simply a distortion of some genetic gifting, talents that are skewed by the pollution of our world and the structure of modern society, as suggested by Thom Hartmann: "Certainly, most of society is set up to reward farmer-like behavior. Our schools are still based on an agricultural model of long summer vacations left over from past times when the children were needed to bring in the crops. Stability is cherished, but job hopping and other forms of social instability are viewed as alarm flags to prospective employees or spouses."[5]

I am becoming increasingly convinced that what we label as impulsive, distractible, and restless, are actually inherent gifts of spontaneity, vigilance, and energy. These qualities are greatly hampered by the effects of sin in the world. For instance, the sin of greed has had a role to play in damaging the health of our minds. Too often the food industry has blatantly disregarded health concerns in their product development for the sake of "profit." Just look at all the unnecessary chemicals we eat because the food industry wants to make their product look, smell, and taste better through chemical means for the sake of making money. As Patrick Quillan states in his book *Healing Nutrients:* "Forty percent of middle class American children are severely malnourished, and adults fare far worse, upwards to 90%."[6]

Just think, that statement was written before the FDA gave approval for one food company to infuse some popular foods with "fake fat." This product has already proven to have negative side effects, such as cramping and diarrhea. Putting this product in foods makes no sense. Our brains have all those unnecessary manufactured chemicals with which to deal. It doesn't take a scientist to figure out that our chemically laced foods are affecting our brain's ability to perform at an optimal level. Unfortunately, when considering the food industry, there's no way to measure how extensively the sin of greed has interfered with healthy brain activity.

Even our educational system hampers these gifts. Interestingly enough, most of the famous individuals mentioned earlier were targeted as "different" because they couldn't perform well within the dictated confines of the educational system. Many of them dropped out of school in the early grades, while some gave up entirely after a few months in the established school environment.

An emphasis has been placed on the importance of a child's ability to sit still, pay strict attention, and achieve academic excellence at a very early age. An emphasis on rote textbook learning has made public education difficult for a substantial amount of individuals. The system functions like a "king" who has placed unfair requirements upon all of us, with disregard for different capabilities. Each and every human has a gift from God, but our world's various cultural practices often hinder their expression by perceptions of what is "normal."

By now, perhaps, you are coming to the same conclusion as me. ADD-type metabolisms are as old as the Bible and have only been exacerbated as "unfit for society" in recent centuries. Actually, if we'll view these traits as genetic gifts, we can easily see them at work in the lives of many of our Bible heroes. For instance, if we look at the life of David, we find that the kind of instincts we now associate with ADD were characteristics that enabled him to survive many catastrophes. His entire life reflects an individual who was inspirational, spontaneous, energetic, vigilant, and prone to take great risks.

The youngest of eight sons, David encountered a great deal of rejection from his parents as a young lad and was sent away to tend the sheep in a dangerous place (Ps. 27:10). As a young shepherd, he fought with a bear and a lion resulting in their death. He learned to become quite a marksman with his slingshot by which he eventually took on the giant, Goliath, despite the mockery of the Israeli soldiers who laughed at the young boy's reckless zeal.

The musical talent he developed as a young man flowed so expressively and spontaneously from his inner being that it became a therapeutic ministry through which King Saul received relief from tormenting demons (1 Sam. 16:23). When King Saul turned against him, he lived the perilous life of an outlaw, dwelling in caves and sojourning through the hills and valleys. He associated himself with debted, distressed, and discontented wanderers who became his followers and friends.

After becoming king, while bringing the ark of the covenant back into Jerusalem, he was leaping and dancing with all his might in a plain linen ephod, rather than displaying the behavior and dress expected of his kingly role. This caused his wife Michal to despise him in her heart. When she confronted him with this "vulgar" behavior, he replied, "I will become even more undignified than this, and I will be humiliated in my own eyes" (2 Sam. 6:22). After rejecting David's carefree, unrestrained, sincere worship of God, Michal lived a life of barrenness. David's immense record of noble deeds and splendid accomplishments were contrasted strikingly by his moral failures. These were clearly marked by impulsivity, a weakness common to modern ADDers. Yet, he is remembered for his genius and his unquenchable passion for God. David's relationship with God was the rudder that steadied his soul, as revealed to us by the Psalms that he wrote.

His son Solomon was "blessed" with similar qualities, having an incredible knack for creativity, spontaneity, and hyperactivity. Perhaps in heaven we can ask any of his seven hundred wives who are present what it was like living with this energetic man. Consider Jacob, Elijah, Daniel, and others who had talents which might now be called symptoms of a disorder. Many of these legendary individuals were people who continually sojourned, surviving not only by the providence of God, but according to the gifting of God within them. These gifts were displayed in things like high energy, spontaneity, vigilance, and a disposition willing to take great risks. Such traits enabled them to survive the harsh and dangerous elements of unknown and often hostile territories.

I wonder how many of the Israelites were comfortable with the prospect of leaving Egypt to follow Moses out into the unknown wilderness. The Book of Exodus contains multiple passages in which the people complained about the discomfort and constant toil of traveling. Perhaps it just wasn't in some of them to live as a nomadic tribe in the desert for forty years. I'm curious to know how that generation explained how it took forty years to make a two-week trip to the next generation.

Moses' battle with Pharaoh over the release of the Israelites from Egypt was charged with a spectacular intensity. His entire experience was a visual extravaganza that we picture in our minds when reading about them. Think of the dramatic scene when Moses approached the burning bush that never extinguished. All of us are familiar with the incredible feats of God exhibited through the ten plagues of Egypt displayed with God's special effects. During the flight from Egypt, Moses and the people of Israel were being led by a cloud by day and a pillar of fire by night. I can just see the children peering out of their tents at bedtime, looking with awe at the evidence of God's presence. My mind races with the visions of things like the water gushing out of a rock, the manna from heaven, and the time when the quail were sent by God for food.

A life of danger, peril, and bizarre events filled his forty years of wandering in the desert with a swarm of people who constantly irritated him with complaints. Moses ultimately became so agitated by their murmuring that he disobeyed God and impulsively struck the rock twice for water, instead of speaking to it as he was instructed. What a mistake that was! Because of this blunder, he was prohibited from going into the Promised Land.

I'm also reminded of Joshua and Caleb who were sent by Moses from the Desert of Paran with a group of men to explore the land of Canaan, which God had promised to them (Num. 13). They discovered a land "flowing with milk and honey," rich in produce and every good thing. Unfortunately, it was also filled with mighty warrior people whom their ten comrades reported to be as giants. Joshua and Caleb insisted on taking the Promised Land with abandon. The whole Israelite assembly wanted to stone them for their dangerously crazy idea. Yet, they seemed to be of the same genes as their leader Moses, who also lived on the cutting edge of high-risk experience.

One of my favorite New Testament ADD types is the impulsive, distractible, risk-taking Apostle Peter. Many important truths were explained to us as a result of Peter's spontaneity and willingness to take risks. In Matthew 14 we find Peter impulsively challenging the Lord to prove it was Him walking on the lake by bidding Peter to walk on the water.

Then in Luke 22, we have the sobering Last Supper of the Lord with His disciples. He foretold His imminent betrayal and also prophesied to Peter about his upcoming trial of faith and personal failure. Without weighing the matter and considering Who was prophesying, Peter refutes the Lord's words by proclaiming that he was ready to go to prison and even die for the Lord. The Lord then proceeds to tell Peter that before the rooster crows he will have denied knowing the

Lord thrice. Any person who is ADD is particularly sensitive to the tears of Peter when the cock finally crows to confirm the Lord's words. They, too, are prone to blurt out what's presently burning in their heart without being cognizant of their past behavior patterns and what is entailed in carrying out their words. This is another rich passage which dramatically illustrates the Scripture which states, "While we were yet sinners, Christ died for us" (Rom. 5:8).

In John 21, we read about Peter's all night fishing excursion with some disciples. Suddenly, the risen Lord appears on the seashore. When Peter realized it was the Lord, he threw his outer garment on and impulsively jumped out of the boat. He quickly swam to shore to be the first to greet the Lord. His passion and zeal were rewarded with the awesome discourse between him and the risen Christ concerning pastoral love and service in life. This text is often found at the center of many sermons because of its rich content.

The perception of Peter as "a poor fellow who was always doing offbeat things" is actually how people continue to perceive these types of people today, who are now referred to as ADD. It would be to our advantage to recognize that these are the kinds of individuals who shake and move things into place for us. They are, indeed, as valuable to us as the farmer types who provide us with a sense of stability and security.

I must also mention that there is a host of farmer types in the Bible as well, who were steady, focused, and calculating in their approach to life. An especially dearly loved one, by the name of Noah, spent one hundred years building a boat (and it wasn't for fishing). He was referred to as "a man of the soil" (Gen. 9:20). In the massive ark he had methodically constructed, he, his family, and a multitude of creatures rode out the great flood. Afterwards, he stepped out into a new world and proceeded to plant a vineyard and establish a homestead for his family, rather than explore the vast terrain in search of life's wonders and new stimulating experiences.

Isaac was also a homesteader type who cared for others and provided stability. He reopened the wells of his father Abraham, not being very successful at pioneering new ones (Gen. 26:18). He seemed to have no real need or drive to change things and was not adventuresome in nature. Job and Samuel were a few others who were steady individuals that had a knack for "staying on task" and appeared as pillars in the midst of unsettling times. These individuals were gifted differently from the earlier mentioned hunter types, but equally valuable in their place in history.

With these things in mind, it would be easy to become a defender of people who are gifted with ADD-type talents. How dare anyone call these symptoms a disorder, illness, or a deficit! Yet to go on the offensive and begin attacking the whole ADD arena, which has become quite large at this point, seems unwise and detrimental.

One such individual is the author Thomas Armstrong, who recently published a book called *The Myth of the A.D.D. Child*. He attacks ADD with a vengeance: "A.D.D. does not exist; these children are not disordered. They may have a different style of thinking, attending, and behaving, but it's the broader social and educational influences that create the disorder, not the children."[7]

I've had a hard time getting people with ADD past the first three chapters of Armstrong's book because of his "attack" approach, although I agree with many of his thoughts. Part of their reaction is due to the fact that ADDers are very sensitive, having been rejected and hurt repeatedly by what people say. Once past the accusations, his fifty suggested ways of improving behavior and attention span in children without the use of drugs, labels, or coercion, are of tremendous value. They would be helpful to any child, not just those with what is currently considered ADD.

I prefer to take the approach of Thom Hartmann. I prefer to encourage and educate those already diagnosed with ADD. I would like to help them reshape their thinking. From this vantage point, those looking into the condition for assistance will find hope and help. They will understand more about the chemistry with which they have been born and how God can help them to use it in a very productive and positive way. I don't find it necessary to become an anti-ADD activist. Medical and scientific advances are moving along so rapidly that in another twenty years, ADD will probably have an entirely different name, or be nonexistent as a condition!

A positive approach automatically brings people together within a nurturing framework, as so clearly proven in Thom Hartmann's CompuServe "ADD Forum" through which people, via computer, share helpful tips and encouraging words of advice. Within this atmosphere, people are encouraged to reach previously unattained heights of achievement, developing their gifts and abilities. This aspect of camaraderie among

ADDers is no different from that of parachurch organizations such as M.O.P.S. (Mothers of Pre-Schoolers), the Promise Keepers men's organization, the AGLOW women's organization, single's groups, youth groups, etc. These kinds of support groups pull people in similar circumstances together and are vital in our journey through life, giving us strength, inspiring the development of our gifts, and helping us see things about ourselves where, perhaps, we have been blinded or ignorant. It is no different with ADD types of issues, except that I haven't begun an ADDers for Christ group—yet (although I do have a newsletter I've begun distributing for Christians dealing with ADD called "The ADDminister," which is listed in the resource section at the back of the book).

Personally, I don't think Christ intends for us to enter these "issue" or "need" groups and camp there permanently. I believe He desires them to be stepping stones in our development of character. Through these groups, we can learn to reach out to individuals in similar situations. Just as I probably wouldn't continue in M.O.P.S. when my children are in high school, I doubt that I'd be deeply entrenched in ADD issues once it's served its purpose.

The journey of life isn't meant to be issue-oriented but Christ-oriented with issues moving in and out of our lives for the purpose of reshaping our attitudes. The many issues we face in life can help us to develop Christ-like character, renew our thought processes, and guide us into union with Christ. It is unfortunate when people get so absorbed in an issue that it becomes the exalted banner over their lives. This life is about learning to love God and others, as Jesus clearly told us in Matthew 22: 37-40. "Love the Lord your God with all your heart and with all your soul and with all your mind. This is the first and greatest commandment. And the second is like it: Love your neighbor as yourself. All the Law and the Prophets hang on these two commandments." We must be careful to keep that end in mind and not get caught up in the means we use to get there.

In summary, we are now challenged to re-shape our perception of ADD symptoms. We need to see beyond the stigmatism to the positive side of this condition, recognizing that there is hope and help. The quality of our experience with Christ in this life can be greatly enhanced as we develop more understanding and grow in our appreciation of differences. To accomplish this, we must tackle two predominant mindsets which greatly hinder us.

The first being that ADD is some kind of disease and acknowledging that its presence in any way cruelly "sentences" us to a life of disability and dysfunction. It is not something to be feared or dreaded, but investigated and appreciated for the positive impact the study of it can have on our lives—improving relationships, personal esteem, and improving child-rearing practices.

The second mindset is that the common symptoms of being impulsive, distractible, and a risk taker are external expressions of underlying God-given abilities. We must fight the urge to be judgmental of adults or children with these traits. We must look beyond the behavior. These individuals

are not simply "irresponsible," but are better
viewed as pioneers, hunters, movers, and shakers.
They provide vital elements needed for pursuing
new territories and ideas for the settlers, farmers,
and stabilizers to inhabit and develop.

Clearly, many of them have secondary destructive behavior patterns. Yet, as with an architectural structure, we shouldn't condemn the whole
building because there's some damage in one part
of the structure. Rather, we should appreciate the
building for its intended useful purpose.

With these two mindsets behind us, we can
now approach the issues of ADD with an open
mind and a willingness to tackle behaviors with
new zeal, hope, and faith in God's guidance.

David prayed:

> I cry aloud to the Lord; I lift up my voice
> to the Lord for mercy. I pour out my com-
> plaint before him; before him I tell my
> trouble. When my spirit grows faint within
> me, it is you who know my way. In the path
> where I walk men have hidden a snare for
> me. Look to my right and see; no one is
> concerned for me. I have no refuge; no
> one cares for my life. I cry to you, O Lord;
> I say, You are my refuge, my portion in the
> land of the living. Listen to my cry, for I
> am in desperate need; rescue me from
> those who pursue me, for they are too
> strong for me. Set me free from my prison,
> that I may praise your name. Then the
> righteous will gather about me because of
> your goodness to me. (Ps. 142)

5. Shape of the Clay

Yet, O Lord, you are our Father. We are the clay, you are the potter; we are all the work of your hand.
—Isaiah 64:8

What makes one human vessel different from another? First and foremost, as indicated by this Scripture, we are fashioned with specific design by our Creator. Many texts confirm this: "Before I formed you in the womb I knew you, before you were born I set you apart" (Jer. 1:5), "This is what the Lord says—he who made you, who formed you in the womb, and who will help you" (Isa. 44:2),

> For you created my inmost being; you knit me together in my mother's womb. I praise you because I am fearfully and wonderfully made; your works are wonderful, I know that full well. My frame was not hidden from you when I was made in the secret

place. When I was woven together in the
depths of the earth, your eyes saw my
unformed body. All the days ordained for
me were written in your book before one
of them came to be. (Ps. 139:13-16)

Our inward parts are fully assembled in the
heart, mind, and purpose of God before they ever
appear in the flesh.

Although God continues to influence our formation once out of the womb, there are many
other factors affecting the outcome of our lives,
which is the topic of this chapter. When any one
of these elements function in a negative manner,
they can generate undesirable behaviors, which
mimic ADD symptoms—such as impulsivity, emotional disturbance, and restlessness. It is therefore
essential that we look into our surroundings and
make sure our environment isn't the primary
source of our troubles. Even when someone has
an ADD metabolism, other areas of influence can
keep them out of sync with life when not recognized and corrected.

Many parents know this to be true. While
Ritalin and other pharmaceuticals help their ADD
children academically, they continue to have dis-
turbing behaviors outside of school. Sometimes,
simply considering natural life experiences can
expose sources fueling negative conduct. As Don
Williams so clearly points out in his book *Jesus and
Addiction,* our problems are not only the result of
sin in our lives. To think this way, he says, "cen-
ters on our personal responsibility. It doesn't
consider the contributions that heredity and environment, or nature and nurture, have made to
the human condition."[1] It is these external factors
we want to consider.

For starters, parents have more of a role in the shaping of lives than they realize. I know this to be a fact from having over ten years of instructing and counseling parents as a children's ministry director. Most parents don't realize the depth of involvement they have in molding and shaping their children's lives. Author Anne Ortlund does a good job pointing out the human factor in molding the clay of a life in her book *Children are Wet Cement*.

> . . . your child is in process, as a person. Every eight days he gets a new layer of skin. Every eight years every cell in his body has become new. Look at that child right now: since this time yesterday he has three million new blood cells. He's growing; he's changing. He's wet cement! Set the habit patterns of his life. You can't make your child—God does; but you can feed him input. If you don't his friends will, and the television will, and movies will . . . And he'll either be improving constantly by the godliness and truth of your fresh input, or he'll keep repeating over and over what he was before, and deepening bad habits or going to worse ones.[2]

Parenting books say that babies are born with a built-in genetic code. Within that genetic code is a broad spectrum of predispositions, from personality traits to biological traits, having both strengths and weaknesses present at birth. This theory is mentioned in an article of the *Orange County Register* by Jim Detjen entitled "It's All in the Genes." He states, "Some scientists think genes will be discovered that indicate whether a person will be tall, intelligent, shy, physically coordinated, musically talented, outgoing, sexually aggressive, or, perhaps, naturally disposed to criminal behavior."[3] The idea of biological predispositions is the theme of author Steve Arterburn in his book *Hand-Me-Down Genes and Second-Hand Emotions*. In it he states,

> Although we can be predisposed to problems from many sources, none are as controversial as the belief that certain emotional problems are a result of physiology. There is so much evidence of biological predisposition that it is hard to see why someone would doubt that certain emotional problems might stem from inborn physiology and not just as a result of spiritual depravity or poor life decisions. We are all predisposed to one degree or another from a variety of sources.[4]

A parent has the privileged opportunity to recognize personality traits from infancy and influence the health and well-being of a child's temperament from birth. The earlier in life this planned approach of "sensitivity to individuality" is taken, the more obstacles a parent can remove from their child's life, lessening—and at times eliminating—the development of behavior problems. There is a direct correlation between the level of parental commitment to molding their children, and the amount of complexes and disorders which may develop in a child's personality.

Left unchecked, these subtle behavior disorders can become lifetime disabilities. When parents attend to their children with sensitivity to their traits, change is not only possible, it is probable. We all know that it is much easier to change behaviors and perceptions in those who are young. The natural tendency of parents is to "treat all children alike" without giving consideration to their individual differences. This inclination can inadvertently damage their uniqueness, causing personality suppression or distortions, emotional depression, and provide fuel for the development of a stifling poor self-image.

Each child has distinctive needs particular to his individuality. Attending to those specific needs requires parents to remain aware and in sync with their child's day to day experiences. When their personal needs aren't met, children can react by being easily distracted, unfocused, and mentally disengaged—all symptoms which can mimic ADD. (Emotional pain can cause these same symptoms in anyone.) For those children who truly have an ADD chemistry to begin with, a lack of parental nurturing will certainly intensify the negative effects of the condition.

The impact parents have on their children's souls is so profound that it has become an important common practice for both Christian and secular psychologists to examine one's upbringing to find solutions to behavior disorders. Contemporary therapists are keenly aware of the impact that parental involvement has over a lifespan. Each of us is familiar with adults whose lives have been fractured by the effects of their parents' influence. Consider the man who is cold and isolated as a result of having never been told "I love you" or shown any affection by his parents. Still another man regularly asks adults for hugs which is his response to the same lack of affection and care of his parents. I've known several people who struggle to learn friendship skills because their parents made sure they never expressed any emotion to others as a child. How many women, having been abandoned by their fathers as young girls, spend their adult lives seeking acceptance from men out of a deep need for a father figure? How much mistrust resides in others who have never married or trusted men because of their father's unjust physical or emotional abuse of them as a child? Parental failure is rampant, and our society is suffering the effects of it.

The negative side to this awareness occurs when people use it to the point of overkill, embracing a "victim" mentality, trapping their very identity within their pain. Instead of making corrections, forgiving offenders, and moving on to wholeness in Christ, they blame parents, society, circumstances, and spouses for what they are and what they do. Blaming others is a way of justifying responses of hate, anger, resentment, and bitterness, which breeds sin.

Each individual passes through crossroads in life which challenge them to take personal responsibility for the "here and now." Resolving ongoing emotional pain from past hurts requires that we enter into forgiveness. We must come to a place of resolve over the past. Each person decides whether or not they are willing to do that. I have found Christ to be the Great Advocate. When I have brought past issues before Him, He has always granted me release and freedom from emotional damage.

This brings up the influence of family structure on the healthy development of a soul—an institution that has been on a downward spiral in recent decades. In *Newsweek* magazine's Special Edition on "The 21st Century Family," they describe the chaos caused by modern family distortions:

> The upheaval is evident everywhere in our culture. Babies have babies, kids refuse to grow up and leave home, affluent Yippies prize their BMW's more than children, rich and poor children alike blot their minds with drugs, people casually move in with each other and move out again. The divorce rate has doubled since 1965, and demographers project that half of all first marriages made today will end in divorce. Six out of 10 second marriages will probably collapse. One third of all children born in the past decade will probably live in a stepfamily before they are 18. One out of every four children today is being raised by a single parent. About 22 percent of children today were born out of wedlock; of those, about a third were born to a teenage mother. One out of every five children lives in poverty; the rate is twice as high among blacks and Hispanics.[5]

Many of these unhealthy situations are responsible for producing deep emotional and psychological damage in the lives of children and adults. These family environment issues are another secondary cause of symptoms that mimic ADD and will also inflame those which are already present in someone with an ADD gene pool. Thomas Armstrong in *The Myth of the A.D.D. Child* states,

> Some parents simply aren't around as much
> these days to provide the kind of guidance
> and support that is essential to a child's
> emotional development. As a result, chil-
> dren are experiencing an epidemic of
> stress-related and mental health difficulties.
> Nearly 1 million reports of child abuse or
> neglect are recorded each year.[6]

I have personally witnessed this damage in the lives of many children, and it is heartbreaking. A father moving in and out of a child's life without much meaningful input leaves the child feeling orphaned and directionless. Children of divorce who must shift between two households and two families have little sense of security and belonging. Those who are living with a hard-working single parent don't have any sense of family due to the financial stress of the parent. Many children have stepparents who make them feel like an outcast, creating long-term damage to their souls.

Another factor, mentioned earlier, which influences the shape of our lives is our formal educational experience. Just about any adult can remember specific teachers who had a positive effect on his soul while growing up, often remembering the "wonderful feeling" associated with that teacher. Concerning our own children, we can easily observe whether or not a particular teacher is providing a nurturing environment in the classroom or is simply "doing his job" from the rote textbook method. I have heard many stories from parents who are outraged by what is taking place in classrooms. I'm told that one teacher is obviously teaching only out of a need for income, and another teacher yells most of the day to try to control the class.

Many seem to play favorites to students who perform well, not to mention those who present material in the most boring of manners. I have actually had to counsel parents who have had teachers verbally berate their child, use vulgar language, humiliate them in front of their peers, or threaten to hit their child in anger. Many of these instances have been without provocation by that particular parent's child, but stem from frustration in the teacher's personal life.

Besides the interpersonal influence of teachers on a child's life, we have the educational system itself that influences our view of life. This factor may even contribute to the outcome of our lives. In the early development of our formal education system, little consideration was given to different styles of learning. The memorization of communicated information is at the foundation of our school system, but what happens to the visual learner or the energetic child? He becomes a hassle to the teacher, an underachiever academically, a disappointment to his parents, and hopeless. This has a dramatically negative affect on his self-esteem and behavior, often leading to feelings of hopelessness and depression about life.

In the lives of children in which educational difficulties are a focal point, teen-age years of rebellion and irresponsibility are almost inevitable. Parents find themselves puzzled by their child's behavior, and the child usually can't explain why he is behaving as he is.

As I began teaching ADD workshops for Christians, I came across many parents who had nightmarish experiences within the public school system concerning their ADD children. Listening to their stories was literally gut wrenching. Several of them are involved in lawsuits. These parents claim that their children's educational needs are not being met, which is a federal requirement under Federal Law 94-142, Section 504. In one instance, the school principal is accused of illegally removing a child's medical records from his school files in order to prevent the parents from having proof of the school's failure to act according to federal laws.

Another teen-ager is in a vocational school working to acquire his high-school equivalency diploma. He is doing so only because he experienced so much rejection from teachers who couldn't deal with his need for activity and visual stimulation. Many educators refuse to make provision for students who have trouble sitting still for six hours and difficulty taking written tests. The stories of heartache and the damage done to these kids is devastating.

U.S. House of Representatives Speaker Newt Gingrich voices similar complaints about our educational system, its negative effect on our children, and its impact on the outcome of their lives. While addressing the Republican Governors Association in November 1995 he stated that we have

> an educational system which allows kids not to learn and which rewards tenured teachers who can't teach while destroying poor children who are trapped in a process with no hope. . . . Our learning should be lifetime, twenty-four hours a day, seven days a week, and based on the learner, not based

on a concrete building, not based on an education bureaucracy, not based on a profession, but based on the learner.... You got to focus on the learner, not the bureaucrat.[7]

In confronting the lack of sensitivity to individual learning styles in our school system, author Priscilla L. Vail writes in her book *Smart Kids with School Problems*:

Once in school, the athletic child with a weak visual memory sinks in look-say reading instruction. The mathematically powerful student with slow visual-motor integration gasps for air trying to take dictation. The verbal reasoner with a weak auditory system drowns in words in classrooms that emphasize listening. The intelligent child with receptive language disability grasps at straws, trying to learn through reading. The poetic child with visual-spacial confusion loses ground trying to solve math problems by using manipulative materials.[8]

Authors Dr. Rick Fowler and his wife Jerilyn Fowler give further understanding to ADD and education in their book *Honey, Are You Listening?*:

In most cases, people with Attention Deficit Disorder are extremely right-brained. That's one of the reasons that ADD individuals often clash with the majority of the rest of the population. Lefties fit comfortably into our modern world. They maintain schedules and order. They fit seamlessly into the educational system because over these many years the system has been fine-tuned to accommodate and encourage the kind of thinking that happens in the left hemisphere of the brain. If you're a teacher, it's a lot easier to write a bunch of dates up on the board and watch your pupil soak them up than to have to work some kind of hands-on mnemonic to shove those dates into the pupil's memory. Teachers enjoy students who can take on facts and figures like a car takes on fuel at the gas pump and then show off on tests—because that kind of student makes their job easier. But not many students are left-brained enough to absorb information that way. Those who are form the high-performance end of every school's grading bell curve. Guess who fills the other end, the failing end.[9]

These quotes point out the dire need we have to reshape education, but the process seems painfully slow.

I have personally known individuals who have been hindered in pursuing their dreams because of educational adversities. I've seen the excellent teacher struggle because she was hindered in receiving her teaching certificate from the local college because she couldn't pass algebra. I know an exceptionally talented drummer who couldn't pursue his dream of becoming a professor of music because he couldn't pass one of the required courses due to what he called a "mental block" in the subject. I also talked with a school counselor who couldn't become the physician she wanted to because of her difficulty in understanding math. How differently their lives would have turned out if consideration was given to their learning differences and an alternative program was offered to help them fulfill their dreams!

One classic example of this failure in our education system was in the life of Vincent Van Gogh. Van Gogh was a "preacher's kid" whose lifetime goal was to follow his father's example into the Christian ministry. His major area of struggle was in functioning within the educational system, which eventually prohibited him from entering the seminary and pursuing his dream of becoming a pastor. He became a lay minister among a Belgian coal mining region, and developed a thriving ministry among them. When denominational officials visited his work, they dismissed him saying he looked more like a coal miner than a "dignified minister." This led him into a life of depression, resulting in suicide at the young age of thirty-seven. A recent article about his life in the *Last Days Ministry* magazine stated:

> While Van Gogh must be held responsible for his own actions, is it possible that the Church might also be partly to blame? If Van Gogh's story was an exceptional fluke, the answer might be "no." Unfortunately, I have personally met many artists who have felt as abandoned by the Body of Christ as Van Gogh. For a variety of reasons and in various ways, a recurring message was thrown their way: "You don't fit in. You don't look like us. You don't act like us." Rather than encourage, train, and properly channel these individuals, we've discarded them.[10]

In many ways this can be said of the educational community as well. Imagine how differently
Van Gogh's life would have turned out if his educators would have recognized his talents and provided a teaching format suitable to his nature.
Instead, he was criticized and rejected for his
uniqueness. He died in poverty and depression.
Even his artwork wasn't recognized until after his
death, when it was finally understood that he
brilliantly painted through emotional spontaneity, which became known as expressionism.

Not only was education a problem in Van
Gogh's life, but the "crisis" of being rejected by
authoritative denominational officials played a
major role in crippling him emotionally. Although
we don't want to be people who are overly focused on our crises in life, it is important to evalu-
ate our experience with them within the context
of surveying behavior problems.

For instance, a newspaper article recently
addressed the effect that violence and criminal
acts has on survivors in the workplace, explaining
that a crisis can produce long-term damage in
people. "Survivors of violence or criminal acts in
the workplace sometimes suffer long-term emotional shocks that are difficult to overcome, psychologists say."[11] Interestingly enough, within the
article's list of crisis symptoms were ADD-type
behaviors: an inability to control emotions, difficulty concentrating, and moodiness—to name a
few.

This demonstrates the possible connection
between behavior problems and crises experienced
while growing up. It is becoming quite clear to
psychologists that events like divorce, chronic ill-

ness, accidents, deaths, and other traumas have lasting effects on people and their behaviors, and more so on children who are in the process of drawing conclusions based on what they experience.

Other factors that I group together as "basic cycle needs" are things like food, rest, and exercise, which our body has need of on a twenty-four hour cycle. These are not often considered when examining ADD symptoms, but a lack of them can cause these symptoms to appear in anyone. I'm reminded of a child in my children's church class who couldn't concentrate because each week he came having not received breakfast, and was distracted by his constant craving for food. In another situation, one of my children ate lunch at such an early period (10:30 A.M.) that by her 2:30 P.M. class she was fatigued, out of resources, and unable to focus on her schoolwork.

Not only is regular eating important, but what is being eaten is equally significant. We all know the fast-food, fast-life pace dominating our society. It is incredibly easy to be given over to foods high in sugar content, chemical contaminants, and many other health invaders, without even trying. As I pointed out earlier, our foods are polluted to an overwhelming degree, and it takes extra effort to try to provide sound nutrition in our homes. A poor diet affects us physically, mentally, and emotionally. Prolonged dietary abuse can cause long-term damage to our mind and body. An organization called the Feingold Association gives helpful information concerning the affects of food on behaviors, which I'll list in the resource section of this book. Although this organization is shunned

by most medical doctors as a viable solution to
ADD, for some it has been very effective in resolving behavior problems.

Another basic cycle need is proper rest. Gary
and I have encouraged our children from a young
age to "read and respond" to their body signals,
explaining that it's better to rest when your body
is exhausted than to keep pushing it and risk an
accident or developing sickness from being run
down. At times when our young teens have gone
to spend the night with friends, we've had parents
comment with astonishment when our teens—at
11:00 P.M.—excused themselves to go to bed so
they would have enough energy for the next day's
activities! I am regularly surprised by the lack of
regulation parents place on their children concerning sleep. Obtaining enough sleep is essential
to our ability to be attentive, focused, and at our
optimum level of productivity.

Physical exercise is another basic cycle need of
our body. It not only affects our physical shape,
but has an impact on the chemistry of our minds
as well. This is very important with children. They
need daily physical activity. A child can exhibit
hyperactive behavior just by the response of his
body to a lack of exercise. For adults in midlife,
a lack of exercise can produce lethargy as the
body is coping with degeneration and needs exercise for revitalization. Both children and adults
require regular exercise for maintaining physical
and emotional health.

Other outside influences play a definite role
in the shaping of our souls. This encompasses
entertainment (movies, television, music, theatre,
literature, etc.), friends, church affiliation, recre-

ation, and other outside interests. We are clearly taught in the Scriptures that whatever we yield ourselves to will have an affect on our lives. "Do not be deceived: God cannot be mocked. A man reaps what he sows. The one who sows to please his sinful nature, from that nature will reap destruction; the one who sows to please the Spirit, from the Spirit will reap eternal life" (Gal. 6:7-8).

The simplest applications teach us this principle: horror movies produce nightmares and fear, rebellious individuals as friends produce moral temptations (1 Cor. 15:3), listening to songs about hurtful broken relationships keeps us remembering past hurts, getting overly absorbed in sports will cause the shape of our lives to look like an athletic event, and so on. We should be people who walk circumspectly as the Scriptures say: "Be very careful, then, how you live—not as unwise but as wise, making the most of every opportunity, because the days are evil" (Eph. 5:15-16).

If you have not lived your life in this calculating manner or managed your children's lives in this way, it may sound like a lot of work to you, but I assure you it isn't. Each of us expends a tremendous amount of time and energy each day, and this approach is simply a redirection of that time and energy into life itself. It is about taking personal responsibility for the life (or lives) we've been given, becoming conscious of the import of our actions, words, and deeds. We have a part to play in the outcome of our lives and the lives of our children.

> In a large house there are articles not only of gold and silver, but also of wood and clay; some are for noble purposes and some

for ignoble. If a man cleanses himself from the latter, he will be an instrument for noble purposes, made holy, useful to the Master and prepared to do any good work. (2 Tim. 2:20-21)

6. Developing a Personal Profile

Teach us to number our days aright, that we may gain a heart of wisdom.

—Psalm 90:12

Talking to a professional is an essential part of seeking an ADD evaluation, but it can be quite costly and time consuming if you haven't thought through personal issues ahead of time. Just recently I was talking with a woman who was on her way to a psychiatrist to discuss symptoms that had troubled her for years. She asked me, "What do I tell him? What do I ask him? I don't know where to begin!" In this chapter I want to provide you with information that will help you begin to assess your life, with the goal of developing a personal profile. A questionnaire is included to help you organize life observations. Many times this procedure, in itself, can reveal things that have never

been recognized and can enable people to solve
behavior problems without need of a clinician.

If you have a support group of Christian friends
with whom you can discuss these matters, it will
help you work through the process. In any event,
it will better prepare you for addressing personal
issues in your life, which may save you time and
money, should you decide to talk to a professional
for further assistance. You can also develop a
child's personal profile through the same process.

There are certain "nurturing needs" common
to everyone. That is where we want to begin. As
we look into them, consider what role they played
in your upbringing.

Love

The first and most basic nurturing need is
love. The Bible teaches us about God's love, which
is unconditional and committed. Gary Smalley and
John Trent give a helpful description of God's
love in their book *The Two Sides of Love*. The basic
premise is that this kind of love has "a hard side
that's consistent, purposeful, protective and mighty
with judgment; and a soft side that's compassionate, tender, forgiving and merciful."[1] We also have
the entire 13th chapter of 1st Corinthians, which
gives us a clear understanding of how this love
works in relationships.

Parents should teach children what love is. In
Phil Phillips's book *Helping Your Children Walk With
God*, he states, "The most attractive emotion to
children is the one that attracts adults: love. Children respond to love. They blossom under it. It
modifies their behavior and their character in a
way that is far more potent than giving them in-

formation or a lush, beautiful, secure physical environment."[2] Surveying how well the need for love was met during one's childhood can clarify many behavior issues. Following are some of the essential ways love is revealed through parents.

Affection

From birth, children need to feel the tenderness of love expressed through physical affection, facial expression, words of kindness, and thoughtful deeds. As children become self-sufficient, many parents lose sight of the importance of being affectionate to their children. Acts of affection should be a regular experience within the home. Hugs, pats on the back, and tender looks, all strengthen our self-esteem. Eye contact is an important act of affection. As Christian author Dr. Ross Campbell states in his book *How To Really Love Your Child*:

> Eye contact is crucial not only in making good communicational contact with a child, but in filling his emotional needs. Without realizing it, we use eye contact as a primary means of conveying love, especially to children. A child uses eye contact with his parents (and others) to feed emotionally. The more a parent makes eye contact with his or her child as a means of expressing love, the more a child is nourished with love and the fuller is his emotional tank.[3]

Compassion

Compassion is that aspect of love which makes people feel accepted, secure, and validated as a worthwhile individual. It is expressed through caring acts such as: speaking words of comfort in a difficult time (even crying babies need compassion), parental assurance that the parent will be there for the child in times of need, helping children overcome their frustration when attempting new tasks, and taking time to listen to children share their feelings, no matter what age they are. These acts display not only a sensitivity to personal needs, but a validation of a child's self-worth.

Compassion shown to children by their parents can eliminate many of their fears and prevent the development of complexes, yet it is important that it not be confused with compliance. Compliance is when we become sympathetic to their discomfort and respond by giving in to wrong demands, thereby rescuing them from difficulty. Ultimately, this prevents them from learning the necessary foundational principle of cause and effect, which is vital to successful living—the sowing and reaping principle found in Galatians 6.

Parents who are prone to being compliant usually are that way because of their own upbringing. Since many didn't have parents who focused on healthy child rearing, this generation of parents commonly enters parenthood with a lot of emotional damage, which easily influences their child-rearing practices.

Take me for example. Being the baby of seven children with an alcoholic father and an overworked, preoccupied mother, I received very little attention from anyone. It caused a great deal of damage in my soul, creating a core of worthlessness and instilling within me a survival mentality. One day I came to realize that I had been wrongly dealing with our own youngest child by frequently complying to her every wish and whimper. This was producing some unhealthy attitudes in her. I realized that unconsciously I was trying to make sure the neglect and disregard I experienced as the baby of my family never happened to her. I began to make changes in my interaction with her. Instead of being compliant, I sought to express compassion and understanding for her discomfort, while being decisive in my actions.

Encouragement

Compliments and words of encouragement should be a regular practice of parents with their children. Children develop their self-awareness according to the responses of those around them. While it takes extra effort for parents to find ways to affirm and uplift their children, the impact it has on the development of a healthy self-esteem is priceless. Children need to hear words that affirm them in their uniqueness, which strengthens their self-confidence.

Communication

A parent's presence is important to a child, but regular communication is equally important. Communication is what makes children sense that they're connected to the family and valuable as individuals. It has been lacking greatly in the American family, as so poignantly expressed by author Jacob Aranza in his book *Lord! Why Is My Child A Rebel?*

> This is the first generation that has had total media exposure. Young people cannot remember a time without television. They were reared with TV as baby-sitter, companion, and comfort. Is it any wonder that when you try to turn it off they get

upset? Why should they listen to you? They
have spent many more hours listening to
television than listening to you. Why should
they start now?[4]

Dinner table talks, car talks, bedtime talks, and
anytime talks help to build a child's sense of inner
worth, security, and oneness with the family, keeping them in relationship with the family unit. Parents who relate to their children in daily conversation develop a healthy bond with them which
fills an emotional need. When children feel that
what they have to say is important to their parents, they will not be easily swayed by peer pressure. Knowing that they are loved, accepted, and
appreciated at home, frees them to have more
control in their academic or social relationships,
rather than being driven to please their peers out
of a deep emotional need for acceptance and
personal value.

Instruction

Once children are taught the basics of life,
many parents take a back seat in the instruction
of their children and leave it to others such as
school, the church, friends, and television. Inad-
equate parental instruction during developmental
years is damaging to the well-being of children,
and leaves out a vital element needed for healthy
nurturing. As Deuteronomy 6 implies, parents
should be sharing life instruction with their children in all that they do, naturally sharing from
life experiences during daily activities.

Too often we confuse giving guidance with
providing information, thinking that if we give
children educational "materials," or send them to

events and camps that give instruction, it sufficiently takes care of a child's need for guidance. But "nurturing" instruction, which is so vital to healthy emotional development, includes learning through shared experiences. Textbooks can only give information; it is the application of that information that leads us to true learning. Conversations about what a particular television show (or movie) is really telling us, explaining how outside influences affect us, and giving explanation for what takes place in the home, are all forms of nurturing instruction that help a child develop in a healthy manner.

Security

Since the day that Adam and Eve hid from God in the Garden of Eden, humanity has been plagued with an innate sense of insecurity. Many people still carry around that shame, covering themselves with "fig leaves" to hide the shame of their condition. A person who is controlled by such deep insecurity ultimately becomes controlled by their surroundings, grasping for anything that will fill the void within. By the grace of God we are able to receive personal security through our relationship to Jesus Christ. Parents can fill that need in the lives of children by providing stability in the home. Many things contribute to the sense of security in the home. For instance, repeated rhythms and cycles provide us with a sense of security.

These are experienced in things like regular mealtimes, regular bedtimes, family devotions, family worship, and annual traditions. These practices provide us with a sense of security and belonging. The many Jewish feasts instituted by God have given longevity and generational strength to Israeli families partly because of the security and sense of belonging that they inspire.

Children from divorced homes who travel between two households have a particularly difficult time feeling secure internally. The general instability of the situation is multiplied if neither of the parents ensure that the child has what they need when traveling between homes. They may get to one home and wish they had remembered to bring something from the other home and vice versa. In these situations it is very helpful if the parents make sure the child literally has two homes with the things that make his life feel normal. Arriving in a home that has his toothbrush, clothes, recreational apparatus, and other things with which the child identifies with "home" will help to retain some sense of rhythm and security.

Following is a questionnaire about your childhood to help you look at the issues presented in this and the last chapter. Each paragraph has multiple questions on a particular issue. You'll need to have a pad of paper and set aside some time in a quiet place, praying for God's illumination on your life before beginning to answer them. Once you have thought through these questions, fill out the subsequent graph. It will help you assess where environmental factors are causing behavior problems for you. Remember that the goal is to identify where external influences might be producing ADD-type behaviors (i.e., distractibility, impulsivity, restlessness), before looking into the biological profile of the condition.

For some people, correcting the problems uncovered through developing this profile might result in eliminating the symptoms that appear similar to ADD. If an ADD biology is present, resolving these secondary issues will serve to lessen the symptoms, making it easier to manage biological patterns without emotional hindrances. For those of you who are ADD, this questionnaire could be tedious (or worse boring), so I'd advise you to just tackle one paragraph at a time. Think about those answers for a few days before moving on to the next one. If you thrive on structure, pick a day of the week and commit to answering one set of questions each week on that particular day until you finish all sixteen.

It is truly important that you take time to consider these issues so you'll have a better foundation for understanding yourself. Just try to remind yourself that there are things more dull in life than this questionnaire! In the long run, you'll be glad you did it.

Personal Profile Questionnaire

Did you receive much affection from your parents? What was your general experience with affection from others? Was it only given when you performed well, or was it a natural part of your family experience? How do you feel the level and quality of affection in your upbringing continues to impact your life today?

Recall some of the difficult times you experienced growing up, namely, problems at school and with friends. Did you receive compassion from your family when you needed it? Or did you have feelings of isolation and loneliness from their lack of concern? Do you continue to be affected by the level of compassion you experienced from your parents today? How?

Did your parents let you get away with everything, being compliant to keep you from causing disruption at home? Or were there rules and guidelines you were asked to follow? How do you feel about how your parents related to you?

Were you encouraged as a child by your parents, teachers, or other adults? Did you feel loved and appreciated for who you were, or did you feel a lot of pressure to perform in a certain manner in order to receive encouragement? How can you see these issues affecting your life today?

Was there a strong line of communication between you and your parents while growing up? Did they listen to what you had to say, and show an interest in your opinions? Do you feel your ideas are important to others? Are you a good communicator or a poor one? What do you feel contributed to your present level and style of communication?

Were your parents the primary source of instruction in your life? How did you come to learn things? Are you fearful about learning things concerning yourself? Do you avoid learning because it makes you feel like you don't know anything? Why would that happen?

Did your parents give you a sense of security in your life, or were things always run haphazard and without concrete rhythms? Do you have trouble feeling sure of yourself as an adult? If so, why do you think you feel this way?

Were you negatively compared to others as a child, or were you accepted and appreciated for your individual traits?

What type of diet did you have growing up? Were concentrated sweets, fats, and chemicals a daily part of your food intake? How do you feel your current eating habits affect your life?

Did you get a lot of exercise as a child? Do you get any exercise as an adult? How do you feel when you don't exercise? Do you view exercise as a stressful activity or stress-relieving activity?

What was your experience with education? Did you enjoy school, your teachers, your classmates? Why?

Did your parents make sure you had enough sleep as a child, or was there little attention given to the need for rest? How do you think that affected you then and now?

Did your parents keep you living in the fast lane, or did your family life provide times of reading, resting, and relaxation? How do you think this affected you? Does it continue to influence you as an adult?

Consider what negative things were a part of your family life while growing up: addictions, attitudes, behaviors. Were any of your parents' problems reproduced in you, and have you reproduced them in your children? What are you doing about it?

Review any crisis you may have experienced growing up such as accidents, traumas, deaths, illnesses, divorce, moves, or other difficulties. In what ways were you personally affected by these events? Do you feel they caused emotional damage that affects your perception of life and relationships with people?

What is your relationship with God? Do you personally spend time with Him on a consistent basis? Do you see yourself living as a disciple of Jesus? Or are you distant from Him personally and relate to Him only within religious practices and events?

Assessment Graph

Circle the number that you feel is your level of experience. It should not be according to how you feel you should be, how others perceive you, or what Scripture instructs you to be, but what you know to be a true assessment. The first set are about your childhood, and the second set are about your current experience.

Circle the level of experience you had with these elements in your upbringing.

1. Affection

Little 1   2   3   4   5   6   7   8   9   10 Much

2. Compassion

Little 1   2   3   4   5   6   7   8   9   10 Much

3. Self-esteem

Little 1   2   3   4   5   6   7   8   9   10 Much

4. Family communication

Little 1   2   3   4   5   6   7   8   9   10 Much

5. Parental instruction

Little 1   2   3   4   5   6   7   8   9   10 Much

6. Sense of security

Little 1   2   3   4   5   6   7   8   9   10 Much

7. Appreciation of your individuality

Little 1   2   3   4   5   6   7   8   9   10 Much

8. Quiet family activities (reading, resting)

Little 1   2   3   4   5   6   7   8   9   10   Much

9. Exercise—physical activity

Little 1   2   3   4   5   6   7   8   9   10   Much

10. Positive education experience

Little 1   2   3   4   5   6   7   8   9   10   Much

11. Proper rest—sleep

Little 1   2   3   4   5   6   7   8   9   10   Much

12. Communication with God

Little 1   2   3   4   5   6   7   8   9   10   Much

13. Sweets, fats, and chemically treated foods

Little 1   2   3   4   5   6   7   8   9   10   Much

14. Exposure to parents' addictions

Little 1   2   3   4   5   6   7   8   9   10   Much

15. Amount of traumas/crises

Little 1   2   3   4   5   6   7   8   9   10   Much

Circle the current level of experience you have with the following elements.

1. Affection

Little 1   2   3   4   5   6   7   8   9   10   Much

2. Compassion for others

Little 1   2   3   4   5   6   7   8   9   10   Much

3. Sense of self-worth

Little 1   2   3   4   5   6   7   8   9   10   Much

4. Ability to communicate

Little 1   2   3   4   5   6   7   8   9   10   Much

5. Desire to learn

Little 1   2   3   4   5   6   7   8   9   10 Much

6. Sense of security

Little 1   2   3   4   5   6   7   8   9   10 Much

7. Appreciation of individuality

Little 1   2   3   4   5   6   7   8   9   10 Much

8. Quiet activities (reading, resting)

Little 1   2   3   4   5   6   7   8   9   10 Much

9. Exercise—physical activity

Little 1   2   3   4   5   6   7   8   9   10 Much

10. Respect for authority

Little 1   2   3   4   5   6   7   8   9   10 Much

11. Proper rest—sleep

Little 1   2   3   4   5   6   7   8   9   10 Much

12. Communication with God

Little 1   2   3   4   5   6   7   8   9   10 Much

13. Sweets, fats, and chemically treated foods

Little 1   2   3   4   5   6   7   8   9   10 Much

14. Attachment to addictions

Little 1   2   3   4   5   6   7   8   9   10 Much

15. Amount of traumas/crises

Little 1   2   3   4   5   6   7   8   9   10 Much

In any of these items, numbers 4 through 6 reflect the median, indicating that you probably weren't deeply influenced by these factors. In item numbers 1 through 12, if you circled below 4, it would be beneficial for you to think about how

the lack of nurturing in these areas may be causing you behavioral problems. Take time to review
numbers that are marked on the low end and
think about how the lack of nurturing is affecting
your behavior today. In items 13 to 15 the reverse
would be true—having above 6 could cause negative behaviors (review these in the same manner).

Having answered these many questions, you
may feel like you've taken your life apart piece by
piece, and are left feeling scattered and unsettled.
This is a natural reaction, since you've suddenly
faced many serious issues concerning the core of
your being. Gary has often commented that some
psychologists can be good at taking a person apart,
but have little success at putting them back together again. This is where a relationship with
Christ comes in. Ultimately, only He can put our
lives back together, heal our hurts, and help us
understand how to make corrections. He alone
knows us "inside out," why we're the way we are,
how we were created, and how we respond to our
environment. Because of this, I want to conclude
this chapter by giving you some spiritual guidelines to help you process the results to the questionnaire and assessment graph.

Oftentimes when we discover things about ourselves or our children for the first time, we can
easily react with discouragement or regret over
years of being bound by things we never recognized, or years of failing to properly nurture our
children. Recently, discouragement fell on an older
friend of mine who suddenly realized her Christian life had been tainted by isolation and a lack
of outreach to others. She felt terrible regret until
I told her, "You need to realize that many people

go to the grave in the condition you were in. God has blessed you greatly."

I was speaking to her out of personal experience. I was quite upset when I realized that I have an ADHD chemistry that was never recognized in my childhood. I recalled the years of struggle, hardship, and difficulty produced by these symptoms. I thought about how different my life would have been if I had been given the tools to understand my metabolism and avoid the pitfalls of my brain type, which I am quickly learning to overcome. I had to get before the Lord with my anger and allow His love to show me the blessing of my new insights. Laying my feelings of condemnation, regret, and anger on the altar of mercy enabled me to receive the healing He wanted to perform in my heart and mind.

If you are struggling with some of these feelings, go before the throne of grace and receive His love and encouragement. Tell Him how you feel, and ask Him to help you be healed from the pain. He cares about your feelings. The Book of Psalms reveals to us that crying out to God is an acceptable, life-giving practice. He wants the "real you," not some religious, mindless robot. God is opening your heart and mind up to bring new life into it. It's unfruitful to stay depressed about the past when the future is filled with opportunity. Release your depression and pain to Him, and He will lift you up.

Some other negative feelings commonly experienced after examining our upbringing are unforgiveness, resentment, and bitterness toward others. These are like a cancer to the soul and must be rooted out. First of all, Christ told us that we

must forgive others before we ourselves can receive forgiveness from God (Matt. 6:14).
Unforgiveness can be a very difficult thing because most of the time we feel we have a right to
it. Christ certainly had a right to it as He hung
there on the Cross, but His response was "Father,
forgive them, for they do not know what they are
doing" (Luke 23:34). This is truly the case with
many of the people who have sinned against us,
and our response needs to be the same as Jesus'
was. Most of the time, those who have wounded
us don't realize they did so, or at least to what
extent they hurt us.

I remember in my early days as a Christian
being deeply wounded by someone very close to
me. Each time I got around this person, I was
extremely upset and angry, feeling justified in my
emotions. Yet, I realized that if I didn't forgive
this individual, God wouldn't forgive me for my
own failures. So I began telling the Lord daily
that I was forgiving this person in my mind, choosing with my will to forgive him, but that God
would have to change my heart.

After several weeks of addressing this in prayer
each day, I suddenly saw this person and had no
emotional reaction. I was so thrilled that God had
taken the forgiveness I was choosing in my mind
and moved it down into my heart. Entering into
forgiveness truly breeds freedom within our souls.
Holding on to unforgiveness brings nothing but
more heartache, torment, and grief into our lives.

Besides proclaiming forgiveness with our will,
we can take steps to make reconciliation with those
who have wounded us. This is not accomplished
by verbally attacking someone for what they did

to offend or hurt us, but by beginning with an attitude of love. "Our relationship is valuable, and I want it to grow. Can we talk about some things that have been difficult for me? I want to know whether I've done anything to offend you in our relationship." We are all guilty of failure and need to know that our failures aren't the end of the world. It's when we cover up our failures, refuse to face them, and avoid dealing with them that they become a problem in our lives. Christ died to absorb our failures, but we have to acknowledge and release them to Him before they can be erased.

The primary step necessary in addressing revealed hurts and weaknesses is setting a course of action. Just as I mentioned about taking steps to correct my interaction with the baby of our family, we must plan to take steps to correct what is out of alignment in our lives.

For some people it might be dietary change (e.g., your level of sugar or caffeine intake might be causing your hyperactivity). In other cases, there might be a need to integrate physical exercise into the schedule (e.g., a lack of exercise could be causing your mind to be easily distracted because of poor circulation). Perhaps you've recognized that there is a lack of rhythm and cycle in your home. Simple adjustments in household practices can make a world of difference, and a lack of rhythm can cause restlessness in anyone.

No matter what the issue is, it will require a change in attitude and a willingness to take responsibility for the here and now. We are each responsible for our words, actions, and responses regardless of external influences. Each one of us "must all appear before the judgment seat of

Christ, that each one may receive what is due him for the things done while in the body, whether good or bad" (2 Cor. 5:10).

These steps toward change should not be made by our own effort but by God's design under His direction. We get into terrible trouble by running our lives without consulting Him first. This requires a commitment to regular times of reflection and prayer before the Lord, seeking His face. Begin by taking the list of answers to the questionnaire and assessment graph and going over them in His presence one by one. Ask God to show you what to do and how to begin making changes that will bring correction in your life.

It is His desire to bring redemption to every area of our lives, but we must take steps to examine our lives with a desire to know what parts are in need of redemption. He is willing, able, and eagerly desires to assist you in your journey through life.

If these surveys have caused an emotional crisis for you, and you feel overwhelmed and unable to cope with the amount of issues uncovered, seek out a spiritual coach. A church counselor, pastor, Christian psychologist, or Christian health care professional can help you sort through things and develop a plan to begin walking out of the past damage done to your soul. Always remember, God is with you and has promised to never leave you nor forsake you!

> So do not fear, for I am with you; do not be dismayed, for I am your God. I will strengthen you and help you; I will uphold you with my righteous right hand. (Isa. 41:10)

7. An ADD Profile

A simple man believes anything, but a prudent man gives thought to his steps.

—Proverbs 14:15

I began to notice individuals who seem to fit the ADD profile everywhere. The entertainment industry spotlights these kinds of people. Sometimes I catch myself laughing while watching a television show or movie when I see adventuresome characters rich in ADD spontaneity and high-energy. Think of what it is we've loved about the characters portrayed in shows like "I Love Lucy," "Gilligan's Island," and "Dick Van Dyke," that's kept them in syndication for years. If you haven't seen public television's "Bill Nye the Science Guy" you're missing out on one of the best educational science shows for ADD types. I would have loved to have him as a science teacher while growing up.

When working on a school homework project, I looked at the many historical characters of our Wild West, thinking how they were individuals who would easily be pegged as being ADD in modern society, fitting the profile to a T. Think of characters like Calamity Jane, Buffalo Bill, Annie Oakely, and Pecos Bill and you'll see what I'm getting at.

Although these kind of characters can prove to be a problem for others, they have qualities we seem to enjoy that actually contribute to our appreciation of life itself. There's no doubt I've come to enjoy a new sense of their value in our world and how they seem to keep things moving along, and I pray you will too.

At this point, let's look at more specifics of what is currently known about ADD traits. In the first chapter, I listed for you the current criteria for diagnosing ADD in children and adults. Both sets of criteria clearly state that for the symptoms to truly stem from a biological condition or disposition, one must have several of them, frequently encounter them, and have experienced them persistently over time (i.e., not just during a time of crisis). Considering those facts is an important part of looking into the possibility of having biological ADD. It's also valuable to remember that it can be experienced to varying degrees as stated by Thom Hartmann:

> ADD is not an all-or-nothing diagnosis. There appears to be a curve of behaviors and personality types, ranging from extremely-non-ADD to extremely-ADD. Although there has not yet been enough research in the field to know the shape of

this curve, it probably resembles a bell curve, with the majority of "normal" individuals falling somewhere in the center, showing a few ADD-like characteristics, and a minority (perhaps somewhere around twenty-thirty percent of the population) being split up on the two extreme ends of the spectrum.[1]

Not only do the degrees of experiencing the symptoms vary, but the manner in which individuals respond to the symptoms varies as well.

A classic example of how differently people can respond to the condition can be seen in the area of disorganization. This is one of the most common traits of people with ADD. For instance, this symptom has not presented itself in my life outwardly. On the contrary, I am extremely organized and able to focus on developing, initiating, and bringing to completion tasks and events. I've even had people ask me how I could consider myself ADD when I'm so organized. The truth is that if I don't have a schedule, day runner, plan, and list, I have trouble getting things accomplished.

Just because I have all those tools doesn't mean I'm organized but that I understand my dire need of them to function well. In other words, my way of responding to the lack of internal structure is by gravitating to organization, while someone else doesn't resist the disarray but simply "free falls" their way through each day. At times, I've actually enjoyed doing some of this "free falling" myself, but I still have a strong tendency to cling to organization. This example demonstrates how differently individuals can respond to ADD, the two responses to the same symptom being quite different.

This idea is conveyed in the code of the DSM-IV criteria, which shows how differently ADD can present itself in individuals, particularly in the area of hyperactivity. Our thirteen-year-old son can appear very docile to others, but he is actually quite hyperactive, often displaying very subtle body movements. On the other hand, our eight-year-old daughter expresses her hyperactivity in an obvious manner, with a lot of expression and physical movement. At one point during her ADD evaluation, she climbed up onto the testing table without even being aware she was doing so. Here again are two people who are hyperactive that present their hyperactivity in different manners. Of course there are also people who test ADD who have no hyperactivity whatsoever.

Such fluctuations have made it difficult for medical professionals to accept ADD as a genuine disorder. After all, most medical conditions appear similar from one individual to another (e.g., measles are measles), while ADD can present itself in an endless variety of shapes and manners, making it seem almost elusive in nature to clinicians. The fact that an exact cause of ADD remains unknown continues to make it an unsteady diagnosis for doctors to promote. Thom Hartmann states this in his book *ADD Success Stories*:

> The National Institutes of Mental Health have shown that the brains of people with ADD have a different type of glucose metabolism, or at least a different rate of blood flow, from those without ADD. This only

validates the neurological/physiological basis of ADD, but doesn't explain what it is, how it works, or where it came from. Similarly, researchers at the University of Chicago believe they've come close to isolating the gene responsible for ADD, but they can't say exactly how that gene affects the brain, or how or why it came to be a part of our genetic makeup.[2]

All of this may sound very confusing, but a further look into the current hypothesis of brain function can give some concrete understanding to what probably takes place in the brain of a person with ADD. These findings have helped me tremendously. As I became mindful of them, I was able to detach myself emotionally from my past patterns (and the patterns of my children) and look at them from a biological standpoint. I was enabled to make adjustments in my thinking and change situations, producing very positive results.

I want to share with you the discoveries about brain function that helped me the most in my quest to understand how the activity within the brain affects behaviors. The information that had the greatest impact on me is explained in the final chapter of Drs. Hallowell and Ratey's book *Driven to Distraction* called "A Local Habitation and a Name." As I read this chapter, I regretted not having read it first because of the clarity it gave me in sorting through behavior issues. I will quote from their book and synthesize the information as I did while reading it.

To begin with, I was impressed by how incredibly complex the attentional system of the brain is.

The attentional system involves nearly all
structures of the brain in one way or another. It governs our consciousness, our
waking experience, our actions and reactions. It is the means through which we
interact with our environment, whether that
environment is composed of math problems, other people, or the mountains on
which we ski.[3]

Because of the complexity of this system, each
person's individual experience takes on unique
expression. Furthermore, a natural supposition is
that if the attentional system isn't functioning
efficiently (the suggested hypothesis with ADDers),
it can impair one's reactions, perceptions, and
behaviors.

Drs. Hallowell and Ratey liken such impairment to different cars in need of a tune-up, each
having their own specific need.

The vastness of the attentional system par-
tially accounts for the variation of ADD
"types." Where one individual needs an oil
change, the next needs spark plugs replaced. Where one individual is withdrawn
and overwhelmed by stimuli, the next is
hyperactive and can't get enough stimuli.
Where one is frequently anxious, the other
is depressed. To compensate, each devel-
ops his or her own coping strategies that
developmentally add to, or subtract from,
the brain's various subsystems. So Mr. A
becomes a stand-up comedian, and manic.
Ms. B becomes an architectural wizard with
obsessive-compulsive traits. Their offspring
becomes a sculptor and a stunt pilot. None
of them can balance their checkbook. And

all of them wish they had more time in the day.[4]

Learning about this helps us understand that a person's mind might not give ample attention to events and circumstances, which can muddle thought processes and create behavior difficulties. When this understanding is applied to relationships, it creates new compassion and insight, breeding tolerance for people's shortcomings. Gary and I experienced this with our ADD children. We became more sensitive to their forgetfulness and inattentiveness to our requests, replacing family conflict with mutual cooperation.

Recognizing these traits in adults, I've become less judgmental of their behaviors as well. I used to get really irritated by people who would talk endlessly without recognizing disinterest or time limitations of those around them. I'm now much more sensitive to the fact that these individuals (whether ADD or not) really aren't cognizant of the fact that they're the only one's absorbed in the conversation. When I first began studying this condition, I found that I often would repeat things when my mind was racing, because I would quickly forget whether or not I said something. One night when I had put our two daughters to bed, I was thinking of a million things that I had to do while telling my husband to go tell the girls good night. I turned to leave and then turned back to tell him the same thing again, because I wasn't sure I had actually spoken the words out. He pointed out that I appeared to be nagging. It suddenly dawned on me what had just taken place and, for once, I was able to explain my irritating behavior and apologize.

Since then I have learned to become more focused in my communication. With Gary's new understanding, he has become a source of support for me and helps me recognize when my mind begins to get in one of those crunches. From these examples, it's plain to see how understanding behaviors in light of brain function is a real source of help in relationships at any level.

As I mentioned earlier, the discoveries about frontal lobe activity are quite important as verified in studies done by G.J. Chelune in 1986.

> According to this hypothesis, many of the symptoms of ADD arise because the brain loses its ability to put on the brakes sufficiently. This is due to disturbed inhibition in the cortex, or outer layer, of the brain. Without cortical inhibition, the brain fails to block inappropriate responses and fails to send out appropriate inhibitory messages. According to Chelune's frontal-lobe hypothesis, the cortex of the frontal lobe is where the action is—or isn't—in ADD. Inhibition breaks down; impulsivity and hyperactivity rise concurrently.[5]

Other studies mentioned point to this same conclusion, including the recognition of decreased blood flow to the right hemisphere of the brain. "The right hemisphere generally controls our so-called executive or decision-making capacities, our visual-spatial abilities, and our ability to process many sources of stimuli simultaneously."[6] In other words, a deficit in this region can produce symptoms associated with ADD like disorganization and inattentiveness.

A reference is also made to the work of Patricia Goldman-Rakic whose studies point to the fact that a deficiency of function in the frontal lobe would affect working memory and

> could cause many of the clinical manifesta-
> tions of the syndrome, since working
> memory controls our ability to review our
> past experience, evaluate our current ex-
> perience, and plan for the future. Rakic
> vividly describes what would happen if
> working memory were to fail: the world
> would be viewed by the brain as a series of
> disconnected events, like a series of unre-
> lated slides, rather than a continuous se-
> quence, like a movie. We have heard the
> world as poignantly described by our pa-
> tients with ADD, sometimes in the same
> words. Life seems discontinuous. There is
> no sense of history. Each new experience is
> met cold.[7]

I easily related to the idea of problems with working memory because of my history of repeating mistakes over and over again. I had always felt a lot of guilt over recurring errors and thought I was either mentally weak, lacked proper formal education, or was just thick-headed. It was quite a relief to recognize that I was simply having trouble connecting experiences and information in my mind, and that I could practice adjusting my thinking to compensate for this, lessening the effect.

Another concept worthy of consideration is the model presented by Dr. Larry Silver who is a known authority on the subject of ADD. His focus is on the activities—or lack of them—in the lower

parts of the brain, which act as a filtering system
for the frontal regions.

> In Silver's model this injured filter system,
> which is regulated by the catecholamines,
> doesn't screen out irrelevant information
> and sensory stimuli as efficiently as it
> should, thereby letting everything that reg-
> isters at the desk of the reticular activating
> system arrive in the rooms of the frontal
> regions of the brain. The individual is
> bombarded, taking care of ten thousand
> guests in a hotel built for one thousand, on
> overload all the time, receiving messages
> about every minute aspect of his or her
> experience. It is no wonder, then, that the
> individual would be distractible or, as Sil-
> ver would argue, inclined to withdraw from
> it all and shut the . . . hotel down.[8]

It is this filter system that is addressed by the
most commonly prescribed medications currently
being used in the treatment of ADD. Those medications activate, or stimulate, the lower region of
the brain for the purpose of regulating the
attentional process of the frontal lobe, obstructing
the reckless flow of messages into the brain. It is
this action that produces such astounding results
for children with ADD who, like Gannon on his
first day with Ritalin, experienced a state of "peace"
in their minds for the first time in their lives.

Understanding brain function has helped me
to understand ADD. Once I read about these
theories, I began to correlate them with the behavior of people with ADD, and I'd like to share
those observations with you.

Various Attention Related Tendencies

• Tend to notice everything going on within visible range; broad peripheral vision.

• Exceptionally intuitive, picking up on emotions, attitudes, and demeanors of those around to the point of being distracted by them.

• Daydream frequently; drift off mentally when engaged in conversation or other activities requiring concentration such as reading.

• Give intense focus to things which are novel; initial zeal wears out once novelty wears off; attracted to current trends, new technology, and gadgets.

• Can remain hyperfocused on things of personal interest for unusually long periods of time, oblivious to surrounding noises and activity.

• View problems or mistakes through a "magnifying glass" hyperfocusing on them, distorting perceptions, producing depression.

Working Memory Related Tendencies

• Unconsciously repeat errors despite their consequences.

• Forgetful of important events, placement of items used daily, normal routines, past learned information, people's names.

• Lack a sense of accomplishment; not cognizant of past accomplishments.

• Insatiable insecurity, need for affirmation, uncertainty of self-worth.

• General disorganization which affects habits and lifestyle practices.

• Intensely overorganized to maintain a sense of order.

Spatial-Time-Logic Related Tendencies

- Anxiety over delays, inconveniences, sudden changes; worry irrationally.
- Put off doing things, unaware of time issues, misjudge time needed either by planning too much time or not enough time—procrastinate.
- Aversion to reading directions and difficulty following them; prefer doing things spontaneously.
- Impatience experienced in communication by speaking without forethought, chronically interrupt others, purchasing of goods beyond means, always being in a hurry or on the go, become easily frustrated when required to wait.
- Lack sense of direction, sense of left or right, klutzy.
- Feel overwhelmed when approaching tasks.

Hyperactivity Related Tendencies

- High energy, gravitate toward thrilling or highly stimulating activities.
- Inner restlessness, constant appetite, or inner cravings.
- Drawn to high intensity situations to release hyperactive nature.
- Drawn to low intensity environments to keep internal hyperactivity under control.
- Prefer challenging experiences over the mundane.
- Compulsive nervous tendencies: nail biting, picking, fidgeting, physical discomfort.
- Excessive talking and focus on self.

Impulsive Related Tendencies

- Easily excited, sense of wonderment about simple things.

- Love to drive, travel, remain on the go.
- Can embark on new ventures in a moment's notice.
- Frequently make snap decisions without planning or proper preparations, acting without thinking things through.
- Always looking for something to laugh about.
- Spontaneous emotions: moody, outbursts of anger, easily swing to emotional extremes.
- Have trouble keeping secrets or confidence.

This is a common profile of thousands of individuals who live as "hunters in a farmer's world." Although this is not nearly a complete list of ADD-related symptoms produced by the brain activity described earlier in this chapter (variations are endless), considering them helped me to look at behaviors in a new light, giving explanation to what had been inexplainable. As with the criteria for diagnosing ADD listed in the first chapter, many of the items I've just listed will ring remarkably true in someone who is biologically ADD, having no other explanation for the symptoms. Again, I want to remind you that the information I am presenting is not intended to substitute a professional diagnosis, but to alert you to possibilities. After all, the first step in attempting to make improvements is to find out what needs to change.

> Wisdom is supreme; therefore get wisdom.
> Though it cost you all you have, get understanding. (Prov. 4:7)

8. Improvement Strategies

Do not be overcome with evil, but overcome evil with good.

—Romans 12:21

A recent article in a local newspaper spoke of a woman named Rebecca Basile, who was conducting an equine therapy lab for fourteen children with ADHD as part of her master's degree program in psychosocial nursing at the University of Southwestern Louisiana. In the program, conducted at USL's riding stables, the children learn the names of all parts of the horse, how to groom a horse, and finally how to ride one.

> "Working with horses gives the medically diagnosed ADHD youngsters a chance to direct fragmented attention spans to an activity that commands their total involvement," Basile said. "They're out of control,

then they get up on a horse and they're in total control," said Basile. Grooming, riding or just being close to a 1,000-pound animal commands attention from even people who aren't ADHD.[1]

"They feel more relaxed," Basile said. "They go back into the classroom feeling better about themselves. And, it doesn't necessarily have to be horses. It could be goats or hamsters."[2]

There aren't very many people who wouldn't benefit from attending a lab of this type. Our society doesn't provide time for many of the simple pleasures in life that contribute to our sense of well-being. People of all brain types suffer mentally, emotionally, and physically from a lack of stress-relieving activities. Many other cultures place a high value on allowing people a chance to "mentally recline" by providing either siestas, tea time breaks, requiring less hours of work, or providing for long paid vacations. Statistically, our nation provides its labor force with some of the least vacation time in all the world. In Juliet B. Schor's book, *The Overworked American*, she states:

> Collective agreements have set an annual leave at 5 to 6 weeks in France, 5.5 to 6 in West Germany, and 4 to 6 in Great Britain. Partly as a cure for unemployment and partly in search of a higher quality of life, European workers have successfully articulated a vision of a more leisured society. That vision is still missing in America, not only in the workplace but in the home as well.[3]

On the same page of this book is a chart from the European Trade Union Institute revealing that most European countries provide more than four weeks a year of paid vacation for all employees, listing Sweden as the highest by providing five to eight weeks off annually.

In what little free time Americans have, modern devices like televisions and computers have replaced the practices of reading, creative hobbies, and outdoor activities. Our trendy forms of "techno-recreation" have contributed to the existence of ADD-type symptoms in much of the common population. They seem to magnify our inability to stay focused. In a monthly report published by Brown University called the *Child and Adolescent Behavior Letter*, an article by learning specialist, Jane M. Healy clarifies this point forthright:

> Should we be concerned about dramatic increases in time children spend with TV and video? Could a heavy diet of visual immediacy and externally directed attention, coupled with reduced time for self-generated play, conversation, reading, and reflection, subtly alter brains and learning abilities? Is a brain that has watched a lot of TV or played countless hours of Nintendo different from one that has not— and would it be harder to educate in a traditional classroom? The answer to all of these questions appears to be yes.[4]

Her article goes on to connect the rapid stimulation techniques used in television with brain responses such as "shorter attention spans, diminished capacity to stick with a problem, reduced comprehension of the complexities of language, and faltering oral expression ('Like, you know . . .'),

and a crisis in listening abilities."[5] With or without
an ADD metabolism, these modern habits can un-
dermine brain function and interfere with the
quality of life. These culturally induced symptoms
are what Drs. Hallowell and Ratey refer to as
Pseudo-ADD:

> What are some of the hallmarks of Ameri-
> can culture that are so typical of ADD? The
> fast pace. The sound bite. The bottom line.
> Short takes, quick cuts. The TV remote-
> control clicker. High stimulation. Restless-
> ness. Violence. Anxiety. Ingenuity. Creativ-
> ity. Speed. Present-centered, no future, no
> past. Disorganization. Mavericks. A mistrust
> of authority. Video. Going for the gusto.
> Making it on the run. The fast track. What-
> ever works. Hollywood. The stock exchange.
> Fads. High stim. It is important to keep
> this in mind or you may start thinking that
> everybody you know is ADD. The disorder
> is culturally syntonic—that is to say, it fits
> right in.[6]

This article makes it plain to see that anyone
can be affected by the things that inflame the
negative side of symptoms for people with ADD.
Likewise, anyone can benefit from looking at the
strategies to improve the life experiences of people
dealing with adverse aspects of the condition. As
stated by an ADD opponent, Thomas Armstrong,
"the reality is that the most successful approaches
for kids who've been labeled A.D.D. are in fact
strategies that have been effective for all kids."[7] I
would only add that adults, as well as children,
may benefit in utilizing these strategies.

One of the first strategies I recommend to anyone dealing with ADD is developing friendships with other people who are ADD. I referred to the value of support groups in chapter 3, but I want to mention them again in the context of being a strategy to help implement change. Organizations like CHADD (Children and Adults with ADD) are formed to help people network with others who are dealing with the same issues, providing new insights and support.

Another network vehicle is the interactive newsletter for kids with ADD called "Brakes." This publication provides a forum for ADD kids (ages 7-14) to communicate with each other. It includes articles written for children by professional experts to answer their questions. The greatest thing lacking in the lives of people I have met who have ADD is a lack of feeling accepted by others. Most of these kids, young and old alike, have been subjected to a lot of rejection throughout their lives.

I also like the concept behind Nancy Ratey's National Coaching Network. She is the wife of *Driven to Distraction* author John Ratey. Along with Susan Sussman, she has begun an organization that provides a coaching service to professionals struggling with the symptoms of ADD.

> Individuals with ADD often know what changes they want to make in their lives, but don't always know how to make those changes. And most importantly, they can get distracted from their goals. The coach can be instrumental in starting an on-going process of defining long-range goals and short-term objectives, and in keeping

the individual on the defined path once it becomes clear. Many athletes and musicians rely on the knowledge and experience of a coach to help them set and achieve goals and make steady progress. Many individuals with ADD also use a coach to help them assess their strengths and weaknesses, learn how to compensate for weaknesses, and develop personal styles that draw on their strength.[8]

Friends who have ADD in common can actually do some simple coaching to each other.

I've experienced this in my relationship with Cindy DeVall, the counselor who tested our children for ADD. Because we're both so versed in the symptoms and are both ADD ourselves, we are able to point out to each other when the condition is clouding our actions. If I get hyperfocused and panicky over things that need to get done before a conference, she'll point out that I'm ADD'n, or magnifying things out of proper proportion, which is a common tendency for people with ADD. With that knowledge I've found I can immediately drop out of the stress into which I had worked myself.

This type of interaction has helped me to become more resistant to stressful thoughts, realizing they're usually unjustified and distorted by my ADD. Although in the past I would eventually resolve anxiety according to my knowledge of the Scriptures, which instruct us not to worry or be anxious, I now have a greater understanding of how to fulfill that instruction by reckoning my anxiety to be a literal distortion in my thought processes. Not only are our worries on earth a distortion of our heavenly reality in Christ, they can also be naturally distorted by our limited perceptions and faulty brain function. This knowledge has encouraged me to be more active in weighing my thoughts before they become a weight in my soul.

I am able to recognize these tendencies in Cindy as well and "coach" her out of a negative expression of a symptom when she's experiencing it, which has been a tremendous asset to her also. I practice this kind of coaching with my children at home. They enjoy "catching me" in an ADD mode and bringing it to my attention. We've all had a lot of laughs and have greatly benefited in giving each other support and encouragement. It has sharpened our ability to communicate, perform tasks, and serve others, resulting in deeper love, appreciation, and recognition of individuality.

Once people take ADD into account for problem behaviors and negative self-perceptions, a re-shaping of one's self-image will begin. One tool which helps to provide stability through this process is the practice of journaling. I would advise anyone embarking on the "sea of change" to journal his experiences in a notebook. The Book of Psalms is a journal of David's personal experiences concerning his faith in God. Being able to look back at lessons learned provided strength in times of difficulty. In many Psalms, David expresses great anguish, but is comforted in recounting the Lord's great deeds, His faithfulness, and unfailing love: "Why are you downcast, O my soul? Why so disturbed within me? Put your hope in God, for I will yet praise him, my Savior and my God" (Ps. 43:11).

Journaling life experiences helps people keep focused on their purpose and goals in life, giving continuity and security. This sense of personal identity is especially valuable to people dealing with ADD. Keeping a notebook by your bedstand will make it easier to employ this practice. Some people do their journaling on computer. Especially if you type well, this will allow you to write more information down in less time.

Even if you only have time for a few sentences, each entry will strengthen your sense of purpose and help to keep you "on task." For children, girls tend to enjoy keeping diaries, particularly if they are making entries while sitting next to Mom who's making hers. Some boys will write in diaries, but many will not. An option would be to put a chart up for them to write down observations of that day: how they felt, how they managed their tasks, and what the victories of the day were no matter how small they might seem.

Many parents use chore and task charts, but in the cases of ADD children, I would also encourage a chart that journals their daily experiences, giving strength to their sense of personal value. This kind of journal chart should be saved instead of erased, for future reference needs.

Examining general areas that are a regular part of life is a simple way to begin improving the quality of life for ADDers. Following are just a few suggested areas to consider when developing strategies for change. Looking at them can help you begin to see what simple changes can be made in your life, or the lives of your family members, concerning some very basic lifestyle practices.

Natural Strategies

"You are what you eat": Work on developing sound nutrition, eliminating whatever fast foods or chemically treated foods you possibly can. Begin placing limits on sugar intake, and develop a general awareness of what's going into the mouth! One woman actually charts each thing her child ingests and then monitors physical reactions in an attempt to eliminate foods that are acting as allergens, causing behavior problems. She claims it's quite successful.

"Use it or lose it": Develop an interest in exercise, whether it be a little league for the kids, or tennis for adults. Make it something enjoyable so it becomes a pleasure and not a chore. Schedule time to burn up some of that energy you have. Some people actually seemed "cured" of many of their ADD symptoms once they began an aggressive exercise program, which is proven to stimulate healthy brain function.

"Recreate don't vegetate": Avoid watching television excessively, playing video games, and surf-riding the computer internet as a form of recreation, but look for things that are of interest to you to spend your time on, such as hobbies, sports, or reading. Help your children develop interests as well and nurture them. If you have that "inner craving for high-stimulation" typical with ADD, try to find constructive things to funnel it into rather than things that waste your time or are destructive in nature.

"Music soothes the soul": Use background music, experimenting with the effects different styles have on you or your children. I've tried this myself and have discovered how different music affects me in various ways. One group's music seems to open the gateway for creativity to flow; another definitely stimulates my energy and helps me handle physical tasks quickly, like cleaning house, and still another allows me to stay focused on a particular task, providing a calming effect.

This isn't a new revelation but has been universally known for centuries and used as a means to influence people in different ways. Music is used to motivate people to make purchases in stores or to evoke a sense of calm in people waiting in a doctors' office.

Parents often use lullabies to help their children become sleepy. In other words, it is a proven strategy for influencing behaviors. Children enjoy the process of researching music's effect on them, too. Be aware that for some ADD people, loud or fast music actually calms them down, similar to how Ritalin (a stimulant) calms down the ADD mind. So, if your child says he or she does homework better listening to the rock band Petra or Whitecross, allow them to do so, giving room for their different body chemistries.

"Faster than a New York minute": Because people with ADD can think of so many things simultaneously, once organized, they can get things done incredibly fast. Without developing organization, only a small amount of the zillions of things they're tackling ever come to completion. Examine what level of disorganization you're experiencing, and look into tools to help you overcome them.

My friend uses a watch with a beeper on it that goes off every day at 3:00 P.M. This beeper reminds her that it's time to be in the office of her private practice. Getting there on time can be a challenge after a full day of counseling at a local high school. She also sets it to beep and remind her when an hour of counseling goes by to keep her on schedule with hour-long counseling appointments. This keeps the typical "time distortion" aspect of ADD in check.

Our society is replete with organizational tools, and it's a lot of fun incorporating them into life. We had a problem with writing down phone messages at our house, so I bought an electronic voice message pad since everyone seems to like electronics better than pens or pencils. If you're unfamiliar with time management tools, just go to the public library and pick up a book on it for a quick education. You could also spend some time at an office supply store. Such places offer a wide variety of products that assist with organizing things. Educational stores provide these for children, too, in the way of charts and calendars. Just watch your budget—it's easy to get carried away!

"Have ears to hear": Review your ability to communicate with others, considering how and when difficulties arise. Consider if those difficulties are resulting from ADD tendencies such as speaking abruptly or without forethought, responding to others reactively from a lack of self-esteem, or communicating out of impatience. Practice being more attentive when others speak. Try to have a stop-and-think attitude before responding. Challenge yourself to allow others to speak more often than you.

When aggravation arises during communication, get in touch with why you're irritated. Don't assume people misunderstand what you're saying or that they don't like you. Perhaps you haven't explained yourself well, or maybe they're just having a bad day. In other words, keep your communication in check. If you're working with children who are ADD, teaching them these principles is very valuable. From a young age, they can become both good listeners and good communicators when given instruction.

At times we've used the television to teach our children about communication, discussing what a commercial is trying to communicate to us, or talking about how someone on a show could have figured things out better if they had just been told all the facts of the story. When talking one on one with them, we go to great lengths to make sure we, and they, are having clear communication about the topic. Misunderstanding others or being misunderstood is a frustrating experience in the lives of many children and adults. It can be corrected with some effort.

These strategies should help you start the process of minimizing the adverse symptoms associated with ADD. If you are an ADD family, make the changes a family affair. It can be a lot of fun for everyone to incorporate new practices in the family. As a family you can begin taking evening bike rides, experimenting with different types of music, or sharing ideas for creating healthy meals. This kind of interaction is valuable for all families, encouraging love, friendship, and a nurturing environment. If you are single, or don't have children, then find a friend who would like to try these changes with you.

Communication exercises are also valuable. I'm sure there are some specific strategies for this out there in "bookland." We created our own as a family. Sometimes we play the "silence game," seeing how long we can keep from making noise. At other times we make a specific effort to take turns talking at the dinner table. With seven of us wanting to share the day's events, it can get pretty hairy at mealtime! For those family members who aren't assertive, they may never get a chance to talk unless some guidelines are laid down.

One unspoken rule of ours is making sure love is communicated to each person during the course of the day. Each person can develop his or her own strategies for each of these natural areas.

If you are interested in examining more in-depth strategies specific to children, I would suggest you look into the fifty strategies provided in Thomas Armstrong's book, *The Myth of the A.D.D. Child*.

The following spiritual strategies are crucially important because they are the fundamental spiritual principles through which the power of Christ can change a life in a supernatural manner.

Spiritual Strategies

"Come near to God and He will come near to you" (James 4:8). Coming near to God has to do with the posture of our hearts, meaning that we choose to become close to Him in our thoughts and daily activities. Because people with ADD are so high energy, it can be especially difficult for them to invest time in a relationship with Some-one they cannot see or feel. There is also the factor of having a distorted view of authority figures, because ADDers are often belittled by parents or teachers, which makes them hesitant to approach the Ultimate Authority, fearing rejection. God has a love that is unconditional, reaching out to each and every individual. He sent Jesus to "reconcile" man to Himself, proving His desire to "accept" us as part of His family. He is all-mighty and desires to touch our deepest needs with His fulfilling love. He delights when we approach His throne of grace. We must make the approach to Him, since He's already approached us by sending Christ and awaits our response.

"My eyes stay open through the watches of the night, that I may meditate on your promises" (Ps. 119:148). In nearly every book I read on ADD, meditation was recommended as a form of developing mental habits of focus, attention, and stillness of mind. For the Christian, spiritual meditation is a profound practice, which produces miraculous results. Some of the most astounding changes I have experienced in my thought patterns and behaviors have been a direct result of meditating in the presence of God.

Although meditation is practiced in a variety of ways in different cultures, for the Christian it simply means to "ponder" or "reflect" on God. This can include focusing on His Word, His ways, His nature, or whatever other thoughts might cross your mind about God. If there is one thing God desires to assist us with, it's our ability to focus our hearts on His heart. This should be a daily practice in the life of any Christian.

Children should be taught, from as young an age as possible, how to quiet their minds and learn to bring them into focus. We've practiced this with our children during family devotions from their toddler years. Young children can be taught the value of having a quiet spirit, resting in the Lord's presence and allowing His love to refresh their hearts and restore their strength. They are remarkably sensitive to the Spirit of God. Once we are practiced on focusing our hearts meditatively on God, we can learn to maintain focus in other areas of our lives. "But I have stilled and quieted my soul; like a weaned child with its mother, like a weaned child is my soul within me" (Ps. 131:2).

"For the word of God is living and active. Sharper than any double-edged sword, it penetrates even to dividing soul and spirit, joints and marrow; it judges the thoughts and intents of the heart" (Heb. 4:12). Because of its inherent power, studying the Word of God is another strategy for people seeking to overcome behavior problems. I'm not talking about studying it for the sake of gaining knowledge, although knowledge of God's Word is to be sought, but I'm referring to studying it for the sake of gaining understanding and making application of that understanding in daily life.

In this way, we experience the Word being "living and active," transforming the very shape of our lives. Contemporary versions assist us with this, such as the Life Application Bible, which provides footnotes to help individuals apply God's Word in a practical way.

"Humble yourselves before the Lord, and he will lift you up" (James 4:10). "Come, let us bow down in worship, let us kneel before the Lord our Maker" (Ps. 95:6). Having a humble opinion of oneself is the gateway for God's Spirit to bring freedom and wholeness since "God opposes the proud but gives grace to the humble" (James 4:6).

The highest expression of humility is the worship of God. It is the abandonment of self into the awesome presence of God. Many people only worship God in the context of congregational meetings, during which personal adoration is primarily expressed inwardly and gestures of humility are constrained by ritual, time, space, or self-awareness in the midst of others. Although congregational worship is a good and scriptural practice, spontaneous personal worship before the Lord is a powerful experience in solitude before the Lord, connecting the created soul to the Creator in a very unique way.

Since spontaneity is so elementary to ADD people, this practice is actually a release of creative energy, acting as a conduit for the power of God to move upon an individual. All Christians should learn to worship God in their private devotions, whether with spontaneous praise or written songs of worship, as a way of embracing humility and acknowledging His greatness. "For this is what the high and lofty One says—he who lives forever, whose name is holy: 'I live in a high and holy place, but also with him who is contrite and lowly in spirit, to revive the spirit of the lowly and to revive the heart of the contrite.' " (Isa. 57:15).

"Do not be anxious about anything, but in everything, by prayer and petition, with thanksgiving, present your requests to God. And the peace of God, which transcends all understanding, will guard your hearts and your minds in Christ Jesus" (Phil. 4:6-7). Imploring God by expressing concerns and making requests or petitions is an important spiritual strategy when desiring to change behaviors and resolve personal issues. God is concerned with our feelings and that which burdens our souls. Through Jesus He told us to love God above all else and to love our neighbor as we love ourselves (Matt. 22:3-39).

However, our generation has tremendous confusion concerning self-love. This confusion creates all kinds of soulish "static" interfering with our ability to love God, love others, and love ourselves. This is particularly true for people with ADD who have a distorted and oftentimes damaged self-perception.

God wants us to love ourselves. We should bring before the Lord the things with which we personally struggle. Things like forgetfulness, failure to follow-through on projects, and lack of self-esteem are important to Him. God will work through circumstances, people, and our hearts to bring healing to us and teach us what Godly love is all about.

If you are dealing with children, there is nothing more important than connecting your children with God through these spiritual strategies. Our family has always practiced them from the time our children were born, and they have made a major difference in their lives. It reminds me of when we had them tested by Cindy DeVall. She was astounded by their level of personal confidence and the security that flowed from them in spite of their being ADD. Having a tendency to take our children's internal strength for granted, I asked her what was so amazing. She explained, "Rarely do I get to see children being evaluated

with ADD with such a sense of personal value.
Your children exude so much love and are so
genuine it's amazing. They don't have any of the
emotional trauma symptoms that I see every day
with children who are ADD. Whatever you're doing
at home has prevented them from being swal-
lowed up by the negative side of this condition."
I then shared with her about our life as Christians
and our commitment to staying close to God as a
family.

Many parents don't know where to begin connecting their children with God. You start by
confirming your relationship with God. You can't
give to your children what doesn't belong to you.
For those who are in a relationship with God, it
is crucial that you communicate the importance of
that relationship to your child. Traditional religion taught us to make our relationship with God
a "personal" thing, keeping it hidden from our
children. As long as it remains personal, your children won't see it as an important part of your life.

They see passion for sports, food, holidays, or
other things, but many children never see the
passion their parents have for God. The Scriptures clearly tell us to share our experiences in
God with our children. From birth they should
see us reading our Bibles, singing songs of worship, praying, and kneeling before Him. Parents
should expect that children will comprehend and
experience God's love and presence, because they
are the seed of the righteous who have an inheritance in God.

They don't have to be intellectually developed
to sense God with their spirits. As the Lord spoke
through Isaiah long ago, "I will pour out my Spirit

on your offspring, and my blessings on your descendants" (Isa. 44:3).

Young children of Christian parents should be viewed more as disciples than as those in need of a radical change. When they are accepted, included, and involved in spiritual activities from birth, they automatically grow from "faith to faith." As our seventeen-year-old son stated recently, "I can't remember ever not knowing God!" This reminded me of David who said "from my mother's womb you have been my God" (Ps. 22:10), which each child of Christian parents is entitled to say.

All five of our children personally know the Lord because we practiced our faith openly in our home and not just on Sunday mornings. They know how real our passion for the Lord is. Each of them has a clear desire to love and serve Him in whatever they do. They each strive for personal excellence in order to bring glory to God and give hope to others. If you would like to gain more insights into connecting your children with God, I would suggest you read Phil Phillips book *Helping Your Children Walk With God*. It is an excellent resource for nurturing and strengthening faith in children.

Whether they are natural or spiritual strategies, these suggestions can greatly improve the quality of life you, or the children you're working with, will experience. Some of the changes you make will be simple and subtle, while others will require a dramatic shift in your current lifestyle. However you decide to approach it, change is within your grasp.

> Train a child in the way he should go, and
> when he is old he will not turn from it.
> (Prov. 22:6)

9. Plotting a Course

Therefore, prepare your minds for action; be self-controlled; set your hope fully on the grace to be given you when Jesus Christ is revealed.

—1 Peter 1:13

As I was preparing to write this chapter, I was reminded of something in Thom Hartmann's *ADD Success Stories* which is pivotal to our discussion. In the chapter "Define Success For Ourselves," he says that success isn't accidental, it's intentional:

> True success is caused by changes based on an understanding of purpose, built on the centeredness of our being. It begins with pain or dissatisfaction with the way life is now, then moves to determine goals, then to develop specific strategies to accomplish those goals. The final step is then to follow through on those strategies.[1]

In the Book of James we read,

> Do not merely listen to the word, and so
> deceive yourselves. Do what it says. Anyone
> who listens to the word but does not do
> what it says is like a man who looks at his
> face in a mirror and, after looking at him-
> self, goes away and immediately forgets
> what he looks like. But the man who looks
> intently into the perfect law that gives free-
> dom, and continues to do this, not forget-
> ting what he has heard, but doing it—he
> will be blessed in what he does. (James 1:22-
> 25)

A few chapters later he also tells us: "Anyone,
then, who knows the good he ought to do and
doesn't do it, sins" (James 4:17). It's not enough
to know the truth. We must act upon it. In twenty
years of giving Christian counsel to people in dire
straits, one of the greatest frustrations has been
getting people to follow through on the prescribed
course of action. This is often quite surprising,
since they appear all fired up about it and determined to follow through when they leave the
counseling session. We've seen weeks, months, and
years of turmoil continue in the lives of people
who just don't follow through on their verbal commitments.

This is a common problem, which seems to
plague the majority of people. New Year's resolu-
tions, political campaign promises, and Lenten
sacrifices all remind us that words are cheap and
the best intentions often deteriorate in the face of
self-gratification. Our commitments might also deteriorate because of the way we react to situations
or people. Many times we allow these situations to

crowd out what we are all about and what we have determined to do in life.

Practical application of knowledge has been at the core of the Hebrew culture for centuries. The Hebrew's concept of education was founded on the premise that information is only learned when it is personally encountered, experienced, and applied. This is reflected in their language which uses one word (lamad) for both "teaching" and "learning." Knowledge was never viewed as disengaged information, but was made an integral part of developing wisdom and understanding through experience and personal encounter.

Jesus taught His disciples in this manner. They didn't spend hours in the synagogue being instructed in a Bible college format but went out and "did the stuff" of God's Kingdom. They assisted Jesus in feeding the hungry (Matt. 15:36), healing the sick, and preaching the good news (Mark 9:6). By the time Jesus had left them, they not only had the knowledge of His ways, but the experience of practicing them. This is more commonly known as being "discipled," or "apprenticed." The very definition of apprentice is "one who is learning by practical experience under skilled workers a trade, art, or calling." Personal encounters with the knowledge we learn leaves lasting impressions that are rarely forgotten.

In our Western world, we have adopted a different approach, teaching detached information in a manner that easily separates "knowledge" from "understanding." This method is very limiting because there is little application of the knowledge being learned, which hinders a person's ability to retain the information. A practical example of this

can be seen in driving a car. All of the textbook
knowledge about operating a vehicle can be easily
forgotten if a person never gets behind the wheel
and drives. It's like going through childbirth classes
for our firstborn. Until I went into actual labor, it
was detached information. Once I experienced
the knowledge I had learned, it was permanently
etched into my memory banks—all nine pounds
nine ounces of him.

Many people assume that because they have
heard something, they really know it. During
counseling sessions, I might give someone specific
information to help them take corrective action in
a situation. Occasionally, someone will say, "I already know that," but their actions speak other-
wise. What they think they know is just nonactive
information. They might claim to know it, but
they certainly don't practice it.

This faulty thinking is at the core of hypocrisy.
Jesus accused the scribes and Pharisees of being
hypocrites because they claimed to have a knowledge of righteousness, but didn't practice heart
attitudes that express what righteousness truly is.
It's not about the knowledge we know, but the
knowledge we own by practice. We have an incredible amount of knowledge in this nation, but
seem to have a low rate of success in causing it to
work in our society. It is clear that this is partly
due to the fact that much of our knowledge isn't
learned within the context of experience.

With that in mind, I want to encourage you to
approach the knowledge you have learned in this
book from the Hebrew method of experience and
personal encounter. The successful road to change
is not solely dependent on the knowledge you

have or the goals or the strategies, but on the final step of following through on those strategies, within the context of experience. Without action, the goals and strategies will remain in the to-do box forever. Many people go to the grave having never functioned at their full potential because they didn't respond with action to the knowledge of the truth about themselves.

One of the biggest problems in facing strategies is staying "on task." I was recently talking to the leader of our local CHADD chapter. Their national newsletter often lists "behavior modification techniques" to help parents make changes at home, and I asked her how effective she felt people were in using them. She said the techniques aren't particularly successful with many people she knows. She thought this was because many of the parents are ADD themselves and have trouble initiating and continuing to practice the techniques on a regular basis.

Oftentimes, they haven't addressed their own ADD troubles, which inhibits their ability to be effective in helping their children. My conversation with her concerned me in light of what I'm trying to accomplish through this book. I've witnessed this problem myself. Many parents with ADD children aren't facing their own condition. They are so consumed by the problems with which their children are dealing that they don't stop to consider how much their children are a reproduction of themselves. Because of this, the symptoms of ADD which continue to present themselves in adults get in the way of them assisting, educating, and nurturing the uniqueness of their children.

Also, people have voiced to me that they don't see where they'll find the time to make all these changes. Frankly, each person "makes time" for what they believe is important. Especially in the mind of an ADD person. People with ADD never seem to have enough hours in the day. I can't tell you the number of times I've counseled people who claim "I don't have time" for whatever the issue is. They say, "I don't have time to spend with my spouse; I don't have time to read my Bible or pray; I don't have time to spend with the children," and so on.

These same people make time for television, sports events, computers, recreation, and other things. It is an illusion to think that we don't have any time, as if time manages us. We are responsible to manage what time we have been granted in this life. Consider the things for which we are willing to clear our calendar. The reality of how much control we have over our schedules becomes evident when we see how our world suddenly stands still when we have the flu for a week.

Each of us has the same amount of hours in our day. George Washington Carver, Thomas Jefferson, Florence Nightingale, Booker T. Washington, and Amelia Erhart accomplished their feats within the same twenty-four hour period that you and I have. They didn't even have a day planner to help them along! Each of these individuals overcame great obstacles in life. What was it that drove them to pursue their many achievements? In studying their lives, I found that they all had one thing in common: a driving inner purpose. They were people who had a sense of their intrinsic value, embracing deep convictions about making a difference. Perhaps they felt a responsibility to make things happen because of their giftedness.

The changes they made in our world speak to us of a determination. We need to ask ourselves what we are for and seek to determine the purpose that guides our actions. When we live for our purpose, we will purposefully live.

Because each person's experience with the symptoms of ADD is different, acting on what has been shared in this book will mean different things for different people. For some people it may require being evaluated for ADD and treated pharmaceutically, or having their children evaluated and treated. In other cases, it may mean making adjustments to circumstances that have been discovered through the questions presented in this book. Some might have to take steps to begin eliminating other factors that could be causing these behaviors as mentioned in chapters 5 and 6. Others might simply want to begin by employing some basic strategies to change behavior patterns. I'm sure it will entail a combination of all of the above in some cases. Whatever approach is taken, whether in the spiritual or natural realm, acting upon your new insights is the key to making them work for you or the children you're influencing.

Simply speaking, many of the changes that will take place will relate to habits. Habits act like a magnet in our lives, which can either pull us toward our goals or away from them. When we decide to develop new habits that are more congruent with our purpose, we often don't realize that their development calls for great commitment. We've experienced this in our home regarding watching television. At one point we decided that the television would not be on during the school week except for educational shows, news, or important event coverage.

Speaking the new rule was easy, while carrying it out required commitment. At one point I gave in and convinced Gary to let the kids watch a show if we had to go out on a school night. Needless to say, they didn't mind us going out at all after that. Once again television became the focal point instead of studies, baths, and chores, so we dropped that practice like a hot potato. Over time, everyone got accustomed to this practice, and the voice of television only calls at us with a whisper. This is only one example of the commitment new habits require of us. As Aristotle once said, "We are what we repeatedly do. Excellence, then, is not an act, but a habit."

If you've decided to begin addressing behaviors that need changing, it's important to understand that you can't correct "everything at once." You have to begin taking little steps or you'll be overwhelmed and just say "forget it" to the entire process. In other words, buy one organizational tool and use it until it becomes a habit, instead of buying ten. This means that even in your strategy, you have to take ADD tendencies into account or you'll burn out in the middle of the whole process.

Likewise, if you're assisting children in developing strategies, you must help them take it one step at a time, encouraging them with every little sign of success. Each effort that our son Gannon made to study for a test or initiate any form of organization was rewarded with praise and encouragement. This gave him the courage to continue addressing the areas of behavior that had once been insurmountable to him.

In the case of our ADHD daughter, she would get overwhelmed when facing multiple tasks like homework. To help her, I would break down the tasks, giving her breaks between subjects during which she could do a variety of things such as have a snack, play a game with me, or go outside for some exercise like roller blading or bike riding. This helped to break the illusion of homework appearing as Mount Everest, enabling her to face tasks with optimism. If you're a parent like myself, who is ADHD as well, creating fun ways to accomplish strategies will be right up your alley. Always remember, for yourself and for your children, you don't have to do it all now but can get everything done by taking one step at a time.

I want to encourage you to take this same approach with all behavior modification. Not only will it be more enjoyable, but your success rate will increase as well. I like looking at it like a jigsaw puzzle, putting one piece into place at a time. If you've ever done puzzles, you know that it's easiest to take one section of the puzzle at a time (the mountains, lake, building, or sky), gathering all the similar pieces and putting them in their proper place. Although all the other pieces lay scattered about, that one section is about to be made right, and so your attention remains there until it's finished. Likewise, continue working steadily on the puzzle of life, bringing each piece before the Lord who is the Master Architect. He delights in directing us to the right piece for the right place if we'll invite Him to.

The easiest way to begin plotting a course of action is to make a list of the problems, and then prioritize the list according to what you feel needs the most immediate attention. For instance, the frustration our daughter was experiencing after school was creating a lot of tension in the house. She started feeling bad about this and was developing a poor self-image. Tackling this problem was the starting place in her case. It took precedence over the fact that she would always forget to do her chores. As we overcame the after-school problem, she was encouraged and began to gain the understanding that, together, we could also find ways to remember our chores, and so on.

In my own experience, once I learned about ADD tendencies, I became aware of problems in my communication with people. Since much of my day is spent interacting with people, this issue was first on the list of things I felt needed immediate attention. I began to practice being less vocal, a better listener, and fully attentive. It took concentration to keep my mind from wandering during conversations, but I found out it was possible.

My heightened awareness of how easily distracted I would become while people were talking to me, actually began to humor me. I never realized it was such a frequent occurrence, because I had glossed over this problem, thinking I was just unable to do anything about it. Little did I know how much power I would receive through this awareness and the action I could take to change it.

I also stopped acting like I had heard what someone was saying, when I had actually drifted off in a conversation (anyone been there?). Instead, I began saying, "Excuse me, I missed the last part of what you were saying because I was distracted. Would you please repeat that again?" While working on communication, I put my problem of forgetful tendencies on the back burner and decided to work on that later.

By just becoming aware of your ADD tendencies, you'll begin to think of new ways of doing things. For instance, one common complaint of ADDers I've come across is their inability to quiet their minds long enough to pray, read, or do tasks which require concentrated focus. The starting place is recognizing that they aren't always so distracted. There are times when they can be extremely focused. This understanding gives them hope that they can learn to focus on something at will.

I encourage people to observe the environment they're in when they or their children are totally focused on something. What is it that helps them remain focused during that time? What were the surroundings? Was their stomach full or empty? What time of day was it? Are there any other clues? If they can do it once, they can learn to do it more often.

Consider these examples: One woman realized that whenever she attempted to meditate, there was noise in the house because of the kids running around. She was tired of yelling at them to be quiet and couldn't seem to shut out the noise. A simple adjustment of changing the time of day during which she meditates made it easier for her to practice quieting her mind and cut down the yelling in her house substantially.

Another person told me that after I made her think about it, she realized there's one room of her house with a skylight that she always seems to get focused and relaxed in. She began to use that room more often when needing to work on something requiring concentration. A child told me that when he was listening to his favorite Christian rock group that he was able to stay focused on his homework more easily. It took some convincing to get the parents to recognize loud music as a quality tool for focusing.

Another child realized that as long as she had a chance to get outside for a while after school, she was much less restless in the evenings. One man told me he finally realized that keeping his office door closed while at work helped him to keep his mind focused. He was surprised to find how much more work he could do without the occasional noise in the hall. Apparently, he hadn't realized the affect this distraction had been causing in his mind, lessening his ability to perform his work.

ADD people who learn about how their brains work and decide to plot a course to eliminate things that have been hindering them have the inbred ability to succeed at doing this. Since they seem to be predominantly right brain, they have the uncanny ability to visualize change and hope for a better day. Acting on new self-awareness, they will experience an expanding freedom to reach for excellence. Of this, I am thoroughly convinced.

In my own experience, I have been amazed time and time again to see God give answers to my questions about how to help my children and make changes in myself concerning ADD behaviors. Sometimes He's answered my questions through a book, a phone call, a letter, a Scripture, or simply by dropping a brilliant thought into my mind. Frequently, He's answered my questions before I've had a chance to ask them in prayer!

I encourage you to consider each day's upcoming events and assess what opportunities each day will provide you with to practice new habits. If you are working with children, consider their daily plans and encourage them to look at things in a new way, a redeeming way. Continue to bring your concerns, or the concerns of the children you're working with before the Lord. Ask for the Lord's help as you seek to develop specific remedies for each area that needs to be addressed. God has a wonderful way of leading us in our efforts to change. Sometimes you'll find that very simple changes make a big difference.

> Know therefore that the Lord your God is God; he is the faithful God, keeping his covenant of love to a thousand generations of those who love him and keep his commands. (Deut. 7:9)

10. Different Strokes for Different Folks

We have different gifts, according to the grace given us.

—Romans 12:6

This final chapter brings us back to the point of recognizing individuality and the variety of paths to ADD wholeness. Each person's uniqueness not only has to do with giftings and abilities, but also with their particular response to things and situations. What works for one might not work for another, and this is certainly true in dealing with ADD.

For instance, any medical doctor treating patients who are ADD will tell you that patients can respond quite differently to the various ADD medications. We experienced this in our family. One of our children responded remarkably to Ritalin, while another did not; he needed a different kind of medication. In the same way, strategies for implementing change can affect people differently, which means you can't always expect the same results as someone else. I've seen people get depressed over this issue, thinking there's something wrong with them because they couldn't get what worked for "Jack" to work for them. We have to get past that narrow thinking and understand that each person has to find out what works for him. I want to share with you stories of people I've come to know during my discovery of the world of ADD and what worked for them.

Nutritional Supplements

Beginning with my family, we came across a company called VAXA, which produces homeopathic neutraceuticals. These products, which include vitamins, minerals, free form amino acids, herbs, and other natural nutrients, are strategically designed to assist the body not only in healing itself, but in functioning at an optimal level. I was put in contact with them by someone who had heard they had some nutritional formulas that were specifically targeted for ADD.

We approached VAXA with a lot of skepticism because of the gimmicky nature commonly found in so-called natural remedies, as well as the fact that VAXA is marketed on a multilevel basis. Gary began to research the issue, the company, and its products, conducting his normal intense research procedures. This resulted in our trying the daily nutritional supplement they have called the Must Pac. Within a matter of a few weeks, Gary and I had dramatic changes. Our minds increased in clarity, we both had increased energy, Gary's sinus condition greatly improved, and we experienced a very tangible sense of well-being. We decided to try the ADD formulas on our children and had just as astounding results. As a result of VAXA, we are, for the most part, now off of ADD pharmaceuticals and doing quite well. We are continuing to make changes in our home to accommodate for the ADD metabolism traits, but now we have few negative symptoms to deal with.

I had the opportunity to speak by telephone with Dr. Gregory Young, founder and president of VAXA, to ask him specific questions about why VAXA was working so well in treating ADD. He explained that the formulas were designed to address the specific dietary and neurochemical deficiencies that are thought to occur within ADD individuals. The nutrients and free form amino acids in the ADD formulas are designed to complement the body's natural calming and balancing agents, which help to focus attention and relieve activity that is either hyper (too fast) or hypo (too slow).

In taking these ADD products myself, I can tell you that they don't give you a rush of silence like Ritalin but, rather, calm the mind down in a very subtle way. VAXA has been a very effective strategy in dealing with ADD symptoms in our family.

I am not suggesting that VAXA is the only nutritional strategy available. In fact, many ADD books mention herbs, vitamins, and other nutrients that can be found at health food stores.

Dietary Changes

Another family, whose mother I've come to know through my conferences, uses the Feingold

Diet with incredible success. Her son had problems paying attention at school and was sporadically hyperactive. After having him evaluated, he was diagnosed with ADD and placed on Ritalin. After two years on Ritalin, he began to develop chronic headaches, stomach aches, depression, and paranoia. Once she learned about the Feingold Diet, she took her son off of Ritalin and began their program. The program is based on a diet that eliminates synthetic colors, synthetic flavors, and the preservatives BHA, BHT, and TBHQ. Dr. Feingold determined that these synthetics interfere with the neurochemistry of the brain, interfering with healthy body function.

By the third week of using the Feingold program, the negative side of ADD was dramatically eradicated. Her son is doing quite well now in school. The entire family of five is on the diet, and she claims that there is much more peace and calm in her household since finding out about Feingold.

Another woman told me of how successful dietary changes were in the life of her son who experienced great difficulty with hyperactivity and distractibility. After trying Ritalin for a few years, she learned about the affect of dyes and food chemicals on behaviors. She developed her own chart to keep track of her son's eating and monitor his physical reactions to food. After eliminating these substances in his diet, she began to watch for what she calls "allergens," meaning foods which produce allergy-like symptoms. Within a matter of months, he was off of the Ritalin and doing quite well.

Schooling and Exercise

One unusually inspiring story was told to me by the father of a young man who had exhibited ADD characteristics from his toddler years. The family moved frequently because of the father's line of work, ending up in Connecticut in the late sixties. His son began attending a school there when he was in the second grade. After his second day at the new school, the father received a phone call from the school asking to have permission to put his son through a battery of tests for his restlessness.

After testing he was diagnosed as having "hyperactivity" and placed on Ritalin. The medication helped him to settle down at school tremendously and stopped the disruption in class being caused by his hyperactivity. Despite the calmness provided by the Ritalin, his son still failed the second grade. After a few years they took him off of the Ritalin because it didn't seem to be helping him enough to warrant taking it any longer. He couldn't seem to function within the structure of the school environment.

When he entered the sixth grade, they had moved to Louisiana where he began attending Holy Cross School in New Orleans. The father expressed to me that Holy Cross is a very unique Catholic school. It approaches education differently than any other school he had seen in that it uses a variety of methods to teach. The father himself had attended the school as a child, and it operated the same way back then. The teaching style wasn't born out of current theories of learning, but had to do with the Christian Brothers' philosophy that every child is different and so you handle each one differently. His son's academic performance improved immediately because of this environment.

The school has always emphasized sports. All students have an opportunity to participate in sports because they offer so many different types. His son began to take up pole vaulting. Pole vaulting is typically geared to tall individuals who are fast and strong. The boy was a "little bitty guy," which didn't fit the traditional pole vaulter mold whatsoever, but the coaches didn't discourage him from pursuing this.

By the time he was in seventh grade, he was on the high-school track team, and he was the second best vaulter in the city! In the eighth grade he placed third place at the high-school state meet. When in the ninth grade, he broke the all-time state record! His father claims that pole vaulting provided him with the opportunity to have an outlet for his energies and attention. As he excelled athletically, his grades continued to vastly improve.

After three years in this atmosphere, the family had to move to another town where he completed high school. Although the new school didn't have the same environment as Holy Cross, his son had learned enough valuable lessons and behavior skills to overcome the traditional setting. He continued to be successful as a pole vaulter in college. After graduating from Louisiana State University, he went on the Pro Tour where he made a successful living as a World Class Pole Vaulter. He competed for ten years in thirty-five countries against guys who were six feet, four inches tall or more, compared to his adult stature of five feet, six inches tall.

Part of his success was due to the fact that even though others were faster than he was, he could "hyperfocus" on placing the pole in the vaulting box and didn't need to slow down at all to do so. He broke many records, including being the first person of his size to ever jump nineteen feet!

His father explained to me that his son's pole vaulting was "driven," and that he was consumed with excelling in the sport. Now, as a thirty-four-year-old man, he is about to graduate from a Louisiana law school. In addition, he has qualified for the fourth time to attend the U.S. Olympic Trials this summer for the 1996 Atlanta Olympic events. The characteristics of his son's ADD are still evident, his father stated, but they are working to his advantage in everything he does.

Another story was told to me by a mother of a young boy who was extremely fidgety. He had a terrible time sitting still at school and was constantly in trouble with his teachers. She began to notice that after he would get a good dose of exercise, he was very calm and settled in his behavior. After realizing this, she approached the school principal and told him of her discovery. She asked that he would be allowed to be a few minutes late to class so he could go outside and jog around the campus for a few minutes. The principal agreed and notified the teachers of this experimental plan. The results were remarkable, having a calming effect on him. The boy was much happier about going to school. He had improved grades and self-esteem. He has since learned to be aware of when he needs to get more exercise.

Medication

Although I've already shared with you how quickly our son received help through medication, I wanted to mention a few other people I've talked to. One woman had a child who "cut up" in class, creating a lot of disturbance in the classroom. This was perplexing to the mother, because the boy was generally very kind and sensitive to others, not malicious or ill-willed in his demeanor.

One day he brought a white lizard in school to show the class. He put it on the shoulder of a girl, which got him into a lot of trouble. After several trips to receive counseling concerning his behavior, the mother had him evaluated. It was determined that he was ADD; and he was subsequently placed on Ritalin, which helped him greatly in the school environment. His mother claims that where he used to be disorganized and messy, he is now much more organized and focused.

A family I know has an energetic son who was just under four years of age. He caused great distraction at home and at school. He wore out everyone around him as they tried to manage his activities and behaviors. The parents had him evaluated by a local physician who diagnosed him as having ADD. The child was put on a low dosage of Ritalin and has had great results with it. He is now much more focused in his pre-school activities and does better at home. His father told me that he's finally able to carry on conversations with his son, who used to be so distracted he couldn't talk coherently.

Counseling

For some people, having a professional counselor who specializes in ADD behaviors has been a key to quickly overcoming emotional problems associated with the discovery of ADD. One woman told me how talking with a counselor who was also ADD helped her to sort through many overwhelming emotions. Another woman sent her son who is ADD to a professional counselor which seemed to help him recover self-esteem and self-confidence. It also made him realize he wasn't some "diseased" individual, but was very special just the way he is.

These are just a few of the many people to whom I have talked who used various methods in solving problems associated with ADD. I suppose one of the most rewarding parts of talking to people about ADD is seeing them freed of self-condemnation and confusion about their identity. A woman I spoke with recently, who found out at age fifty that she was extremely ADHD, told me,

> I was overwhelmed with a sense of relief. I have always tried to be a good person, be active in church work, and do what is right. Yet, I had this constant sense that I was a failure because I couldn't get organized and seemed to be so impulsive. I always felt awful about myself, and it really made my life miserable. Now, I understand why I am the way I am; and I can look out for ADD habits. Many times I can stop myself from doing ADD things before they happen because I've become so aware of how they work in my life. It's been very liberating and has brought me much happiness.

This emphasizes the fact that no matter how old you are, if you're ADD, finding out about it can be beneficial to you. I learned this after sharing a copy of the book *Driven to Distraction* with a successful seventy-eight-year-old businessman who I felt had a lot of ADD traits. He thoroughly enjoyed the book and considered it to be a revelation of his past experiences. I asked him to tell me what he personally experienced in learning about ADD, and he shared the following with me:

> When I recognized that I'm a classic case of ADD, I began to understand the WHY of so many of my actions, both as a child and as an adult. It explained why my Dad used to say that I learned to run before I learned to walk, and why I was seldom able to sit still for long periods of time like my siblings could. It made more sense of my ability to hold a paper route at the age of 8, and soon after began doing janitorial work and mowing yards for several people. At a young age I organized friends to help with the work and paid them a portion of my earnings. While I was in high school, during the depression in the 1920s, I hired a grown man to work for me full time doing yard work!
>
> My low grades in some subjects were probably because of being ADD, while I easily excelled in subjects of interest to me. Learning about the ability of people with ADD to hyperfocus helped to explain why I could become the most quiet and relaxed kid around when reading an exciting adventure book like *Tarzan and the Jewels of Opar*.

I look back and see that I was a good fol-
lower (e.g., in the Boy Scouts), and yet was
a leader as well. Overall, though, I was
mostly a loner when it came to friendships.

Sometimes as a young teenager I would
get in the middle of town on a Saturday
afternoon and hitchhike in all four directions. When I got my first ride I would go
in that direction as long and as far as I
could go and figure I could still get home
by Sunday night. When I would leave home
I would tell my folks that I would see them
tomorrow. When they asked me where I
was going I would tell them that I didn't
know. I think my Dad understood me rather
well and figured I wouldn't get into any
trouble. He somehow knew I just had to
get out and away.

Knowing about ADD helps explain many
things about my childhood. I somehow always knew that I would one day work for
myself, even though I had no idea what I
would be doing. I was one of the kids with
an overabundance of self-confidence and
full of daring deeds, usually just to show
off. I did some bad things as a youngster,
but not necessarily bad enough to go to jail
for if I had been caught. My eighty-eight
year old cousin, with whom I was raised,
told me recently that I was a bad little boy.
I told her that perhaps I was mischievous
but not bad. She insisted that I was a bad
little boy; never mean, but a bad little boy.
Since that remark, I have thought about it
and have concluded that she was probably
right!

Realizing all of the above is probably connected to having ADD has been a great
benefit to me. It answered many of the
questions I've always had about why I did
certain things the way I did them. I now
enjoy claiming I have ADD and the energy
that goes with it. Most of all, at seventy-
eight I enjoy being able to tell my kids:
"Hey, don't fuss at me—I've got ADD!"

As this gentleman demonstrates, we're never
to old to learn something new.

What, then, shall we say in response to this?
If God is for us, who can be against us? He
who did not spare his own Son, but gave
him up for us all how will he not also, along
with him, graciously give us all things? Who
will bring any charge against those whom
God has chosen? It is God who justifies.
Who is he that condemns? Christ Jesus,
who died—more than that, who was raised
to life—is at the right hand of God and is
also interceding for us. Who shall separate
us from the love of Christ? Will trouble or
hardship or persecution or famine or na-
kedness or danger or sword? As it is written; For your sake we face death all day
long; we are considered as sheep to be
slaughtered. No, in all these things we are
more than conquerors through him who
loved us. For I am convinced that neither
death, nor life, neither angels nor demons,
neither the present nor the future, nor any
powers, neither height nor depth, nor anything else in all creation, will be able to
separate us from the love of God that is in
Christ Jesus our Lord. (Rom. 8:31-39)

Appendix

Resources

Suggested Reading Materials

Edward M. Hallowell, M.D. and John J. Ratey, M.D., *Driven to Distraction* (New York: Simon & Schuster), 1994. This book covers attention deficit disorder extensively, giving tips, resources, and practical knowledge.

Thom Hartmann, *Attention Deficit Disorder: A Different Perception* (Grass Valley, Calif.: Underwood Books), 1993. Thom Hartmann gives a very positive, unique, and uplifting profile of the ADD metabolism.

Thom Hartmann, *ADD Success Stories* (Grass Valley, Calif.: Underwood Books), 1995. In this book, Thom Hartmann gives a lot of helpful insights, especially concerning brain function. He also provides proven strategies from a host of individuals who shared with him their ideas about managing ADD tendencies.

Thomas Armstrong, Ph.D., *The Myth of the A.D.D. Child* (New York: Dutton Books), 1995. After a few chapters of attacking the validity of ADD, Thomas Armstrong gives fifty important strategies for improving behaviors in children.

Dr. Rick Fowler and Jerilyn Fowler, *Honey, Are You Listening?* (Nashville, Tenn.: Nelson Books), 1995. Written by Christian authors, this book is about how ADD could be affecting your marriage. It provides insightful suggestions for improving relationships in which ADD is a factor.

Kate Kelly and Peggy Ramundo Tyrell, *You Mean I'm Not Lazy, Stupid, or Crazy?* (New York: Scribner), 1995. Written by and for ADD adults, this book addresses many important issues for the ADD adult, giving tips for coaching, organizing, and managing ADD tendencies.

Priscilla Vail, *Smart Kids with School Problems* (New York: Plume Books), 1987. This learning specialist gives concrete understanding about how differently people learn, providing helpful suggestions about how to cultivate the different kinds of minds in a classroom.

Patricia O. Quinn. M.D., *ADD and the College Student* (New York: Magination Press), 1994; (800) 825-3089. This book gives college and career guidance for students who have ADD, providing resources to help students achieve their potential.

Organizations and Support Groups for ADD

CHADD (Children and Adults with ADD), 499 N.W. 70th Ave., Suite 308, Plantation, FL 33317; (800) 233-4050. This is a national and international non-profit parent-support organization for children and adults with ADD which has groups that meet in nearly every state to discuss ADD issues and concerns.

ADDA (National Attention Deficit Disorder Association), P.O. Box 972, Mentor, OH 44061; (800) 487-2282. This organization provides educational resources on ADD to individuals and support organizations.

Adult ADHD Clinic, University of Massachusetts Medical Center, 55 Lake Avenue North, Worcester, MA 01655; (508) 856-2552. This clinic serves adults, but the medical center also provides treatment and research in childhood ADD.

The ADD Forum on CompuServe (Online, GO ADD) CompuServe Information Service, (800) 524-3388, Representative 464. The ADD Forum operates twenty-four hours a day year round, providing discussion groups, conferences, and resource information libraries.

National Coaching Network (for coaching individuals with ADD), P.O. Box 353, Lafayette, PA 19444; (610) 825-4505. This organization provides a professional forum for people who do coaching for individuals with ADD, providing training, education, and a newsletter to all network members.

Newsletters and Publications

The ADDminister, Generational Publications, P.O. Box 52109, Lafayette, LA 70505. This is author Theresa Lamson's newsletter to assist Christians in their understanding of ADD and related issues.

CH.A.D.D.ER and *CH.A.D.D.ER Box*, 499 NW 70th Avenue, Suite 308, Plantation, FL 33317; (305) 587-3700. *CH.A.D.D.ER:* Biannual magazine which often contains articles by the leading researchers and clinicians for adults with ADD.

The ADDed Line, 3790 Loch Highland Pkwy, Roswell, GA 30075; (800) 982-4028. This is Thom Hartmann's publication, a newsletter "for hunters in this farmer's world."

ADDendum (for adults with ADD), c/o C.P.S., 5041-A Backlick Road, Annandale, VA 22003. A quarterly publication for adults with ADD which features up-to-date information on ADD. It includes insights, interviews, informative articles, and a question-and-answer column.

BRAKES, Magination Press, 19 Union Square West, New York, NY 10003; (800) 825-3089. An interactive newsletter written specifically for children ages seven to fourteen who have ADD. It provides a forum for children to communicate with each other and presents information to help them understand how to function effectively as an ADD individual.

ADDult News, 2620 Ivy Place, Toledo, OH 43613. A newsletter for adults with ADD dealing with a broad spectrum of issues.

Nutritional Resources

FAUS (Feingold Association of the United States), P.O. Box 6550, Alexandria, VA 22306; (703) 768-FAUS. This organization is geared to generating public awareness of the potential role of foods and synthetic additives in behavior, learning, and health problems.

VAXA Neutraceuticals and Homeopathic Supplements, P.O. Box 52109, Lafayette, LA 70505; (318) 233-8024. Nutritional and homeopathic vitamins, minerals, amino acids, herbs, and other sources are combined in VAXA products to address specific body chemistry needs, including those of people with ADD.

International Foundation for Homeopathy, 2366 Eastlake Ave. East, #329, Seattle, WA 98102; (206) 324-8230.

Notes

Chapter One

1. Dr. Edward Hallowell and Dr. John J. Ratey, *Driven to Distraction* (New York: Simon & Schuster, 1994), Preface, X.

2. Ibid., 274.

3. Paul Harvey, "There's Help for Super-Hyper Kids," Syndicated Column, 16 November 1995.

4. Michael Gordon, Ph.D., "Certainly Not a Fad, But It Can Be Over-Diagnosed," *Attention!* (Fall 1995): 22.

5. Hallowell and Ratey, *Driven to Distraction*, 201.

6. Ibid., 199.

7. Thom Hartmann, *ADD Success Stories* (Grass Valley, Calif.: Underwood, 1995), Foreword, xi.

Chapter Two

1. Dr. H. Newton Malony, *Integration Musings: Thoughts on Being a Christian Professional* (Pasadena, Calif.: Integration Press, 1995), 14.

2. Ibid., 9.

Chapter Three

1. Stephen R. Covey, *The 7 Habits of Highly Effective People* (New York: Simon & Schuster, 1989), 24.

2. Thom Hartmann, *ADD Success Stories* (Grass Valley, Calif.: Underwood Books, 1995), 38.

Chapter Four

1. Dr. Edward Hallowell and Dr. John J. Ratey, *Driven to Distraction* (New York: Simon & Schuster, 1994), Preface, X.

2. Thom Hartmann, *ADD Success Stories* (Grass Valley, Calif.: Underwood Books, 1995), 4.

3. Thom Hartmann, *Attention Deficit Disorder: A Different Perception* (Grass Valley, Calif.: Underwood Books, 1993), Introduction, xxiii-xxiv.

4. Gary Smalley and John Trent, Ph.D., *The Two Sides of Love* (New York: Pocket Books, 1993), 51-140.

5. Hartmann, 10.

6. Patrick Quillin, *Healing Nutrients* (New York: Random House, 1987), 43-52.

7. Thomas Armstrong, Ph.D., *The Myth of the A.D.D. Child* (New York: Dutton Books, 1995), Preface, xii.

Chapter Five

1. Don Williams, *Jesus and Addiction* (San Diego, Calif.: Recovery Publications, 1993), 31.

2. Anne Ortlund, *Children Are Wet Cement* (Grand Rapids, Mich.: Spire Books, 1995), 49.

3. Jim Detjen, "It's All in the Genes," *Orange County Register,* 1 January 1992, Section E, 1-2.

4. Stephen Arterburn, *Hand-Me-Down Genes and Second-Hand Emotions* (New York: Simon and Schuster, 1992), 20.

5. Jerrold K. Footlick, "What Happened to the Family?" *Newsweek Special Edition* (Winter/Spring 1990): 16.

6. Thomas Armstrong, Ph.D., *The Myth of the A.D.D. Child* (New York: Dutton Books, 1995), 28.

7. House Speaker Newt Gingrich's remarks to Republican Governors Association, Federal News Service, 1995, 4, 10, 14.

8. Priscilla L. Vail, *Smart Kids with School Problems* (New York: Plume Books, 1987), 147-148.

9. Dr. Rick Fowler and Jerilyn Fowler, *Honey Are You Listening?* (Nashville, Tenn.: Thomas Nelson Publishers, 1995), 9.

10. Denny Gunderson, "The Plight of the Christian Artist," *Last Days Ministries,* vol. 18, no. 1 (1995), 24.

11. Randy McClain, "Coping With Shock," (Baton Rouge, La.) *Advocate,* 12 December 1995, sec. 4H, 1.

Chapter Six

1. Gary Smalley and John Trent, Ph.D., *The Two Sides of Love* (New York: Pocket Books, 1993), 12.

2. Phil Phillips, *Helping Your Children Walk with God* (Nashville, Tenn.: Oliver-Nelson, 1992), 81.

3. Ross Campbell, M.D., *How to Really Love Your Child* (Wheaton, Ill.: Victor Books, 1992), 39.

4. Jacob Aranza, *Lord! Why Is My Child a Rebel?* (Lafayette, La.: Huntington House, 1990), 18.

Chapter Seven

1. Thom Hartmann, *Attention Deficit Disorder: A Different Perception* (Grass Valley, Calif.: Underwood Books, 1993), 1.

2. Thom Hartmann, *ADD Success Stories* (Grass Valley, Calif.: Underwood Books, 1995), 3.

3. Dr. Edward Hallowell and Dr. John J. Ratey, *Driven to Distraction* (New York: Simon & Schuster, 1994), 269.

4. Ibid., 280.

5. Ibid., 276.

6. Ibid.

7. Ibid., 277.

8. Ibid., 281.

Chapter Eight

1. C. Richard Cotton, "Grooming, riding horses helps kids with ADHD," (Baton Rouge, La.) *Advocate,* 26 December 1995, Section B, 1.

2. Ibid., 2B.

3. Juliet B. Schor, *The Overworked American* (New York: Basic Books, 1991), 82.

4. Jane M. Healy, "TV Video Shape the Developing Brain," *Brown University Child and Adolescent Behavior Letter,* December 1991, 1.

5. Ibid., 2.

6. Dr. Edward Hallowell and Dr. John J. Ratey, *Driven to Distraction* (New York: Simon & Schuster, 1994), 191.

7. Thomas Armstrong, Ph.D., *The Myth of the A.D.D. Child* (New York: Dutton Books, 1995), 57.

8. Nancy Ratey, Ed. M. and Susan Sussman, M. Ed., "ADD Coaching Q & A" (Lafayette Hill, Pa.: National Coaching Network, n.d.), 2.

Chapter Nine

1. Thom Hartmann, *ADD Success Stories* (Grass Valley, Calif.: Underwood Books, 1995), 41.

We welcome comments from our readers. Feel free to write to us at the following address:

Editorial Department
Vital Issues Press
P.O. Box 53788
Lafayette, LA 70505

More Good Books from Vital Issues Press

The Basic Steps to Successful Homeschooling
by Vicki A. Brady

If you are a parent already convinced of the moral and intellectual benefits of home education, this book is for you. Working on the premise that home education is a wise decision, Vicki Brady, an expert in the field, provides the reader with a practical, nuts-and-bolts approach to implementing a system of home education. Because of its clear, step-by-step format, this book serves as an invaluable guide for beginner and expert alike in the field of home education. The decision to homeschool is a serious, often intimidating one, but one that serves many families well, if carried out properly. This book will make the decision less daunting, providing home educators with a wealth of knowledge and, therefore, confidence.

ISBN 1-56384-113-4

Big Book of Bible Promises
edited by David England

Designed for children between the ages of 4 and 8, the *Big Book of Bible Promises* is a beautifully illustrated picture book that combines scriptural text with historical works of art. Chapters include: Anger, Love for Others, Obedience, and Patience. *Big Book of Bible Promises* is a wonderful way to help your child prepare for life.

ISBN 1-56384-123-1

Bible Promises for Little Ones
edited by David England

Bible Promises for Little Ones is an educational picture book for children 4 to 8 years old. Parents and grandparents alike will appreciate the educational features of this remarkable book, which include concise application of scriptural truths from the King James Version of the Bible and full-color reproductions of historical art. *Bible Promises for Little Ones* will enrich a child's educational and spiritual development, providing valuable lessons in preparation for the teen and adult years.

ISBN 1-56384-124-X

How to Homeschool (Yes, You!)
by Julia Toto

Have you considered homeschooling for your children, but don't know where to begin? This book is the answer to your prayers. It explains how to find the best curriculum for your children; where to find the right books; whether certified teachers are better instructors than stay-at-home moms; and what to tell your mother-in-law.

ISBN 1-56384-059-6

Anyone Can Homeschool:
How to Find What Works for You
by Terry Dorian, Ph.D., and Zan Peters Tyler
Honest, practical, and inspirational, *Anyone Can Homeschool* assesses the latest in homeschool curricula and confirms that there are social as well as academic advantages to home education. Both veteran and novice homeschoolers will gain insight and up-to-date information from this important new book.

ISBN 1-56384-095-2

Children No More:
How We Lost a Generation
by Brenda Scott
Child abuse, school yard crime, gangland murders, popular lyrics laced with death motifs, twisted couplings posing as love on MTV and daytime soap operas (both accessible by latch-key children), loving parents portrayed as the enemy, condom pushers, drug apologists, philandering leaders . . . is it any wonder that heroes and role models are passé? The author grieves the loss of a generation but savors a hope that the next can be saved.

ISBN 1-56384-083-9

Dinosaurs and the Bible
by David W. Unfred
Every reader, young and old, will be fascinated by this ever-mysterious topic—exactly what happened to the dinosaurs? Author David Unfred draws a very descriptive picture of the history and fate of the dinosaurs, using the Bible as a reference guide. Did dinosaurs really exist? Does the Bible mention dinosaurs? What happened to dinosaurs, or are there some still living, awaiting discovery?

ISBN Hardcover 0-910311-70-6

Conquering the Culture:
The Fight for Our Children's Souls
by David Paul Eich

Remember Uncle Screwtape? He was the charming
C.S. Lewis character who tried to educate his nephew,
Wormwood, on the art of destroying souls. Now, from
a fictional town in Montana, comes a similar allegory.
This compelling book is a valuable source of support
for parents who need both answers and courage to
raise moral children in an immoral world.

ISBN 1-56384-101-0

Legacy Builders:
Dad, What Does Your Life
Say to Your Wife and Children?
by Jim Burton

Today, feminism and changing economics make it
difficult for men to understand their role in a society
that seems to devalue their inherent qualities. Discover how men can build a legacy—and why America
so desperately needs men to understand their role in
the family and society.

ISBN 1-56384-117-7

The First Lady:
A Comprehensive View of
Hillary Rodham Clinton
by Peter & Timothy Flaherty

Is Hillary Rodham Clinton a modern career woman or
an out-of-control feminist? In this compelling account
of her life, the authors suggest that Mrs. Clinton has
been misrepresented in the media and misunderstood by both conservatives and liberals alike.

ISBN 1-56384-119-3

Out of Control—
Who's Watching Our Child
Protection Agencies?

by Brenda Scott

This book of horror stories is true. The deplorable and unauthorized might of Child Protection Services is capable of reaching into and destroying any home in America. No matter how innocent and happy your family may be, you are one accusation away from disaster. Social workers are allowed to violate constitutional rights and often become judge, jury, and executioner. Innocent parents may appear on computer registers and be branded "child abuser" for life. Every year, it is estimated that over 1 million people are falsely accused of child abuse in this country. You could be next, says author and speaker Brenda Scott.

ISBN 1-56384-069-3

Outcome-Based Education:
The State's Assault
on Our Children's Values

by Peg Luksik & Pamela Hobbs Hoffecker

From the enforcement of tolerance to the eradication of moral absolutes, Goals 2000 enjoins a vast array of bureaucratic entities under the seemly innocuous umbrella of education. Unfortunately, traditional education is nowhere to be found in this controversial, strings-attached program. In this articulate and thoroughly documented work, Luksik and Hoffecker reveal the tactics of those in the modern educational system who are attempting to police the thoughts of our children.

ISBN 1-56384-025-1

The Gender Agenda:
Redefining Equality
by Dale O'Leary

All women have the right to choose motherhood as their primary vocation. Unfortunately, the radical feminists' movement poses a threat to this right—the right of women to be women. In *The Gender Agenda*, author Dale O'Leary takes a spirited look at the feminist movement, its influence on legislation, and its subsequent threat to the ideals of family, marriage, and motherhood. By shedding light on the destructiveness of the radical feminists' world view, O'Leary exposes the true agenda of the feminist movement.

ISBN 1-56384-122-3

Getting Out:
An Escape Manual for Abused Women
by Kathy L. Cawthon

Four million women are physically assaulted by their husbands, ex-husbands, and boyfriends each year. Of these millions of women, nearly 4,000 die. Kathy Cawthon, herself a former victim of abuse, uses her own experience and the expertise of law enforcement personnel to guide the reader through the process of escaping an abusive relationship. *Getting Out* also shows readers how they can become whole and healthy individuals instead of victims, giving them hope for a better life in the future.

ISBN 1-56384-093-6

Do Angels Really Exist?
Separating Fact from Fantasy
by Dr. David O. Dykes

Have you ever seen an angel? Don't be too quick to answer "no." For most of us, angels evoke images of winged, white figures frolicking from one cloud to another. But, according to the Bible, angels are God's armored warriors ready to protect His kingdom in heaven, as well as His beloved followers on earth. By citing dozens of fascinating angel encounters, the author presents evidence that angels roam the earth today, protecting and comforting God's people. You might be encountering angels without even knowing it.

ISBN 1-56384-105-3

Journey into Darkness: Nowhere to Land
by Stephen L. Arrington

This story begins on Hawaii's glistening sands and ends in the mysterious deep with the Great White shark. In between, the author finds himself trapped in the drug smuggling trade—unwittingly becoming the "Fall Guy" in the highly publicized John Z. DeLorean drug case. The author recounts his horrifying prison experience and allows the reader to take a peek at the source of hope and courage that helped him survive.

ISBN 1-56384-003-3

High on Adventure: Stories of Good, Clean, Spine-tingling Fun

by Stephen L. Arrington

In the first volume of this exciting series of adventure stories, you'll meet a seventeen-and-a-half-foot Great White shark face-to-face, dive from an airplane toward the earth's surface at 140 M.P.H., and explore a sunken battle cruiser from World War II in the dark depths of the South Pacific Ocean. Author and adventurer Stephen Arrington tells many exciting tales from his life as a navy frogman and chief diver for The Cousteau Society, lacing each story with his Christian belief and outlook that life is an adventure waiting to be had.

ISBN 1-56384-082-0

High on Adventure II: Dreams Becoming Reality

by Stephen L. Arrington

Join the former Cousteau diver again as he travels around the world, revisiting old acquaintances from the deep and participating in dangerous, new adventures. In this exciting second volume of the series, Arrington even explores the underwater lava flow of an active volcano—while it is in progress!

ISBN 1-56384-115-0

Everyday Evangelism: Witnessing That Works
by Ray Comfort

This warm, funny, down-to-earth volume is filled with suggestions on how to reach out to others. Whether you're in a restaurant, at work, or even at the mall, there are many easy, effective, and inoffensive ways to share your faith. As practical as it is entertaining, *Everyday Evangelism* is one book every Christian will enjoy—and refer to again and again.

ISBN 1-56384-091-X

How to Be a Great Husband
by Tobias Jungreis

In marriage, failure is *not* an option. This user-friendly, upbeat guidebook gives men easy, practical suggestions on how to keep their marriages vibrant for a lifetime. Unique features include insightful lists of do's and don'ts and dozens of ideas drawn from a myriad of real-life situations. *How to Be a Great Husband* offers a refreshing approach to the "work" that is marriage, giving husbands invaluable insight on how to achieve success in this most important area of their lives—insight they can apply at the dinner table tonight! Read this book and discover how easy it is to be a "ten" among men.

ISBN 1-56384-120-7

The Blame Game:
Why Society Persecutes Christians
by Lynn Stanley

The liberal media is increasing its efforts to suppress Christian values and religious freedom. At the same time, liberal courts and organizations such as the NEA are working to eliminate religion from American culture. In *The Blame Game*, Lynn Stanley exposes the groups attacking the constitutional rights of Americans to tradition and freedom of religion. Also, she explains what these factions fear from mainstream America and why they seek to destroy it through their un-American system of wretched moral relativism.

ISBN 1-56384-090-1

The Walking Wounded:
A Look at Faith Theology
by Jeremy Reynalds

Is the faith movement saving souls—or destroying lives? After a pastor's wife dies of cancer, he is told that it was due to a lack of faith. A woman in Sweden is so traumatized by the faith movement that she enters a treatment program for ex-cult members to recover. According to a recent study cited by the author, many former faith members appear to have developed severe psychiatric problems from their experiences. Read what he has to say and decide for yourself whether word of faith doctrine is orthodox Christianity or outright heresy.

ISBN 1-56384-076-6

Freud's War with God:
Psychoanalysis vs. Religion
by Dr. Jack Wright, Jr.

Freud's hostility to religion was an obsession: he dismissed all religious belief as a form of mental illness—a universal neurosis—and devoted his life's work to attacking it in whatever form it might appear. No other single theorist has had the impact on psychiatrists, psychologists, and social workers as has Sigmund Freud. Dr. Jack Wright demonstrates how his influence can be felt in such varied phenomena as gay rights, outcome-based education, and the false memory syndrome—all elements of the culture war that rebel against God and religious orthodoxy.

ISBN 1-56384-067-7

In His Majesty's Service:
Christians in Politics
by Robert A. Peterson

In His Majesty's Service is more than a book about politics. It's a look at how real men have worked out their Christian beliefs in the rough-and-tumble world of high-level government, war, and nation-building. From these fascinating portraits of great Western leaders of the past, we can discover how to deal with some of the most pressing problems we face today. This exciting, but historically accurate, volume is as entertaining as it is enlightening.

ISBN 1-56384-100-2

Health Begins in Him:
Biblical Steps to Optimal
Health and Nutrition
by Terry Dorian, Ph.D.

This book is offered as a resource for all those seeking knowledge about how to change their lives in ways that will enable them to preserve and maintain optimal health. Health and nutrition aficionados will also find this volume essential, thanks to the guidelines, scientific studies, and testimonials. Clear, concise, and lively dialogue makes this a very readable directory on foods, food preparation, lifestyle changes, and suggestions for renewal. Terry Dorian, Ph.D. has been a whole-foods advocate for more than twenty years and conducts seminars that teach degenerative disease prevention and cures.

ISBN 1-56384-081-2

Combat Ready:
How to Fight the Culture War
by Lynn Stanley

The culture war between traditional values and secular humanism is escalating. At stake are our children. The schools, the liberal media, and even the government, through Outcome-Based Education, are indoctrinating our children with moral relativism, instead of moral principles. *Combat Ready* not only discloses the extent to which our society has been influenced by this "anything goes" mentality, but also it offers sound advice about how parents can protect their children and restore our culture to its biblical foundation.

ISBN 1-56384-074-X

To Grow By Storybook Readers
(Phonics in Action)
by Janet Friend

The quality of education in America is a major concern, and many parents are turning to homeschooling to teach their children to read. The *To Grow By Storybook Readers* can greatly enhance any homeschooling reading program with gentle Christian instruction. The set consists of eighteen softbound Storybook Readers plus two Activity Books. The *To Grow By Storybook Readers* are designed to be used in conjunction with Marie LeDoux's PLAY'N TALK™ phonics program but will work well with any orderly phonics program.

Complete Set ISBN 0-910311-69-2
Series A ISBN 0-910311-98-6
Series B ISBN 0-910311-99-4

The Truth about False Memory Syndrome
by James G. Friesen, Ph.D.

With his new book on false memory syndrome, Dr. Jim Friesen cuts through all the misinformation being bandied about on this subject. Through harrowing, yet fascinating, case studies—dealing with everything from sexual to Satanic ritual abuse—Friesen educates the reader on the most complex coping mechanism of the human psyche. A pioneer in the treatment of multiple personality disorder, Friesen dispels the myths surrounding FMS and victims of abuse as no tabloid or talk show can.

ISBN 1-56384-111-8